PILLS, SHOCKS & JABS

The Remarkable Dissenting
Doctors of Georgian Bristol

PETER CULLIMORE

Bristol Books CIC, The Courtyard, Wraxall,
Wraxall Hill, Bristol, BS48 1NA

Pills, Shocks & Jabs
written and researched by Peter Cullimore

Published by Bristol Books 2021

ISBN: 9781909446298

Copyright: Peter Cullimore

Design: Joe Burt

A CIP record for this book is available from the British Library.

Cover image: Gaspare Traversi, circa 1753. With the Matthiesen Gallery 1989. © Matthiesen Ltd

Printed by TJ Books Limited

CONTENTS

INTRODUCTION

Pills, Shocks & Jabs was inspired by the man who built our eighteenth century house in Bristol - and went bust doing so. Shurmer Bath (1738-1800), a Quaker businessman, amateur doctor and property developer, featured in my previous book about the history and past residents of Spring Cottage.

Since the publication of *Saints, Crooks & Slavers* in 2020, I've discovered much more about Shurmer Bath's work in the sphere of medicine. In an age when premature death was normal, he practised as an untrained and unpaid doctor, offering free pills to patients with no money.

He was my starting point for this subsequent narrative, which focuses on the social history of medicine in Georgian Bristol. My research made me aware that a surprisingly large number of the city's most prominent doctors and surgeons were also Quakers, despite these religious dissenters forming only a small minority of the population.

The Religious Society of Friends, as they were otherwise known, had faced persecution after breaking away from the established Church of England in the mid seventeenth century. Many Quakers in Bristol later defied prejudice by joining the medical profession and forging successful careers against the odds.

Pills, Shocks & Jabs relates how Georgian Bristol was at the cutting edge of change, in an unregulated system still as likely to kill you as to provide a cure. One example of progress was a medical team who paved the way for their colleague up the road in Berkeley, Dr Edward Jenner, to develop his ground-breaking vaccination against smallpox.

A Bristol Quaker, Dr Abraham Ludlow, helped improve the safety of smallpox inoculation (also known as variolation), which was the method used previously to combat the deadly disease. He then became one of the first

Spring Cottage: one of a number of houses in Montpelier, Bristol, which Shurmer Bath started building in the 1790s, but never completed because of the Napoleonic Wars. He was also a Quaker maltster, philanthropist, amateur doctor, electrical healer and dinner party philosopher.

doctors to offer Jenner's new vaccine to his patients. There are clear parallels with the Covid-19 pandemic and its devastating effects on our twenty-first century world.

Dr John Till Adams, also a Quaker, excelled as a qualified practitioner in several branches of medicine. His wife Ann worked with him until his death, then independently, as a dispensing druggist (chemist or pharmacist, in modern terms). She also treated seriously ill patients herself, with great skill, even though women were excluded from medical training courses.

This book examines in detail the significant contribution of Bristol Quaker medics to improvements in healthcare provision, especially for the most deprived families. However, a lot of shameless profiteering also went on. Even some of the best practitioners were accused of overcharging for medicine, by prescribing far more doses than their patients needed. I've revisited eyewitness accounts of some doctors' pompous manner and outrageous behaviour.

Many of these anecdotes were written down and kept for posterity by a medical colleague at the new Bristol Infirmary, founded in 1736 on a charity basis. The same chronicler, Richard Smith junior, was a surgeon and self-confessed "body snatcher", who dug up and stole corpses for dissection.

Not all the characters chosen were Quakers or other religious dissenters. A few, like Jenner (the son of an Anglican vicar) and Smith, are included in *Pills, Shocks & Jabs* because their stories were too important, or simply too irresistible, to leave out.

However, it's remarkable that so many outstanding medical pioneers emerged from the Society of Friends in the Bristol area. For example, Dr Edward Long Fox rose to prominence in the new field of psychiatry. He designed and ran a radically different, more humane, style of "lunatic" asylum for treating mental illness.

A young Joseph Fry's apprenticeship to a much-respected family doctor helped give him the skills to manufacture chocolate and cocoa. These products, which were advertised as being good for your health, later made Fry's chocolate a household name across the world. However, Joseph started out as an apothecary (part chemist, part GP), and set up a thriving medical practice in the city centre.

Treatment back then was often a matter of trial and error. We'll see how the amateur doctor Shurmer Bath's faith in electricity as a healing agent was shared by some evangelical preachers, including the Methodist John Wesley, and even by some qualified medics.

All these characters were exceptional individuals, while also sharing a common bond from their involvement in medicine and from being religious dissenters with their own distinctive community in Bristol.

Many took the opportunity to join Bristol's lively Quaker social scene. This was a hub for the latest philosophical and scientific ideas, all in a framework of family warmth and shared moral values. It took place in the homes of people living in easy walking distance from each other, concentrated in one particular area of the city.

The queen bee at the heart of it all, who knew everybody in the influential Quaker network, was the diarist Sarah Champion Fox. For half a century she kept a daily record of life, illness and death, social entertainment and deep personal friendships. Her Diary provides another thread to guide our journey through a crucial period of social and medical history in England's second city.

Bristol still had a culture of charity and philanthropy, which to modern eyes sits very uneasily alongside its status then as Britain's number one slave-trading port. Its merchants profited from the barbaric cruelty inflicted on enslaved people. Millions were shipped in chains from Africa across the Atlantic, often to their deaths. Yet this was also the so-called Age of Enlightenment, when minds opened up to progressive new ideas and free thinking.

In the mid eighteenth century the Quaker movement switched from tolerating the slave trade to backing the campaign for its abolition. Meanwhile, Bristol Quakers embraced innovations in science, medicine and education, while still maintaining their traditional piety and sobriety.

Publication of my first book, *Saints, Crooks & Slavers,* coincided with the rapid spread worldwide not only of the Covid-19 virus, but also the Black Lives Matter movement and the toppling of slave trader Edward Colston's statue in Bristol city centre in June 2020.

Shurmer Bath, too, profited from slavery by twice marrying into families who'd owned sugar plantations in Barbados. The events of 2020, harking back to the historical slave trade, therefore gave that book a modern resonance it might otherwise have lacked.

Pills, Shocks & Jabs will strike a chord with many of us who've endured the coronavirus pandemic. Vaccination, in particular, was a hugely important issue two centuries ago, affecting everybody. Now it's become so once again. I've retired as a journalist on ITV Wales, specialising in health. Otherwise I'd have been reporting on daily developments in the pandemic for the television news. The flu pandemic of 1918-1920 caused tens of millions of deaths worldwide. With that exception, our global Covid crisis has perhaps focused more attention on life-or-death health issues than at any other time since the Georgian era.

'Dispensing Medical Electricity' by Edmund Bristow, 1824.

WHO'S WHO

MAIN CHARACTERS

EDWARD ASH (1736-1818)
He served 18 years as Treasurer of the Bristol Infirmary, from 1791 to 1808, and was the eighth Quaker in succession to hold the post. Ash, whose family wealth originated from manufacturing sweet raisin wine, became a major landowner when his wife Elizabeth inherited the Ashley Estate on the north-east fringes of Bristol.

SHURMER BATH (1738-1800)
He was a maltster by trade, but widely known as "Doctor Bath" because of his career as an untrained medical practitioner, giving away free medicine to the poor. Bath was a generous benefactor to local health and education charities and became one of the first in Bristol to treat patients with electric shocks. He twice married into the Dury family, who'd formerly been slave-owning planters in Barbados.

JOSEPH BECK (1721-1793)
The Beck family were close friends of the diarist Sarah Champion Fox. She made frequent visits to their country estate, known later as Frenchay Manor, to spend time with Joseph, his wife Mary and their children. Joseph was a leading subscriber to the Infirmary and an early Treasurer of the Bristol Dispensary. He joined the campaign against the slave trade. The Becks took ownership of the Ashley Estate in 1776. It later passed to their daughter Elizabeth, who was married to Edward Ash.

WILLIAM BRODERIP (1747-1826)
The Bristol Infirmary chronicler Richard Smith singled him out as the worst case of an apothecary grossly overcharging his patients. Broderip was accused of giving them far more medicine than they needed at extortionate prices. He enriched himself enough to build a luxurious mansion as his family home. Broderip made a fortune, but then lost it all through his extravagant lifestyle.

RICHARD CHAMPION (1743-1791)

He came from one of Bristol's elite Quaker dynasties, involved in the local brass, copper and zinc industries. Richard, who was the diarist Sarah's brother, followed two other Champions into the post of Infirmary Treasurer in 1768, when still only 25. He set up the short-lived Bristol China porcelain factory in the city centre, but later ran into financial trouble and emigrated to America.

SARAH CHAMPION FOX (1742-1811)

She kept her Diary for half a century, when illness and death were constantly just round the corner, even in her genteel world. Doctors, therefore, loom large in Sarah's record of social interaction with family and friends in Georgian Bristol. In addition to ruminating about her own poor health, she often visited people recovering from a bad cold or a fever, or stoically facing their "removal" to a Quaker burial ground.

WILLIAM DYER (1730-1801)

Another Bristol diarist, with a more down-to-earth approach, left us his entries for just one year – 1762. William Dyer wrote down the details, often in note form, of his daily working life, both as a professional accountant and as an amateur doctor. He concocted his own medicines and pills from herbal ingredients. Dyer also claimed to have been the city's first practitioner to try electric shocks as a remedy for his patients' physical ailments.

JOSEPH FRY (1728-1787)

He was trained, and practised, as an apothecary in Bristol, before switching to making chocolate, which he claimed was good for your health. Joseph took over the patent for a water-powered machine that ground cocoa flakes to a powder, so creating a smoother breakfast drink. It was the start of a hugely successful family enterprise, which later made Fry's and Bristol synonymous with the world's first chocolate bar.

ANNA FRY (1732-1803)

Joseph's wife, daughter of the apothecary who trained him, took charge of the chocolate business after Joseph died suddenly in 1787. Anna Fry developed a new purpose-built factory in the city centre, run with traditional Quaker standards of moral behaviour and discipline. The couple had been active participants in the local Friends' religious and social life.

WILLIAM FRY (1779-1812)

In the early 1800s young William Fry took over a thriving druggist shop started by his aunt, Ann Till Adams. It stood in Union Street, next to the Fry's chocolate factory. William's parents were John Plant Fry and Hannah Dury, from the former slave-owning family in Barbados linked by marriage to Shurmer Bath. William Fry died in 1812, aged only 33, but his chemist shop kept going for 100 years longer.

JOSEPH HARFORD (1741-1802)

The Harfords were another of Bristol's powerful Quaker families. They'd grown rich from banking and investment in the local metal industries. Joseph Harford was especially influential in charity fundraising for the Infirmary, serving 12 years as its treasurer. In 1788 he also chaired the Bristol Committee petitioning Parliament to abolish the slave trade. However, by then Joseph was no longer a Quaker. He'd transferred to the Church of England to further his ambitions as a Whig politician, becoming the city's Mayor in 1794.

DR EDWARD JENNER (1749-1823)

This country doctor in Berkeley, near Bristol, proved that vaccination gave protection against smallpox, by deliberately infecting a child with a milder form of the disease. His cowpox experiments, inspired by local folklore, eventually led to vaccination being made compulsory for all infants in Britain. The jabs were also introduced across Europe and in America, where President Thomas Jefferson became an enthusiastic advocate. Jenner's name has won new recognition during the Covid pandemic as the historical forerunner of modern vaccines against the coronavirus.

DR EDWARD LONG FOX (1761-1835)

He was a physician specialising in mental illness, who built his own asylum that became a model for national reform. Brislington House was designed to treat "lunatics" more humanely, in the belief that insanity could be cured. Instead of locking up and chaining his patients in barbarous conditions, Dr Fox gave them accommodation comparable to home, but separated by social class. They were allowed exercise and fresh air and treated with kindness and respect - a policy influenced by the psychiatrist's own Quaker moral code.

DR ABRAHAM LUDLOW (1737-1807)

The son of a Bristol surgeon with the same name, Dr Ludlow was one of Bristol's most prominent physicians. He combined pompous arrogance in his appearance with hard work and dedication to all his patients, rich and poor alike. Dr Ludlow ran an extensive private practice and was the family doctor of choice for many well-to-do Quakers, including the diarist Sarah Champion Fox. He provided safer jabs against smallpox for children at a local "inoculating" house and later introduced free vaccinations for the poor at the Bristol Dispensary.

DR THOMAS POLE (1753-1829)

Thomas Pole was already an American scientist and childbirth specialist of international stature when Sarah Champion Fox sold her house to him in St James Square. He moved from London with his family in 1802. Dr Pole was a true man of the Enlightenment, immersed in new ideas on medicine and science. He had roots in Somerset, but his debt-ridden father emigrated to America. Thomas returned from Philadelphia as a wandering Quaker minister and preacher, before becoming a man-midwife and eminent lecturer in obstetrics. Dr Pole's talents also included drawing silhouettes, portraits and exquisite watercolour scenes.

RICHARD SMITH (1772-1843)

He was an accomplished and long-serving surgeon at the Bristol Infirmary. However, Richard Smith junior's main legacy rests with salvaging the Infirmary's early records and writing his often scurrilous biographical memoirs, warts and all, of past medical colleagues. Smith's lurid style and mischievous eye for detail give some of his anecdotes a satirical humour worthy of Hogarth. Best of all are his descriptions of "body snatching" carried out by Bristol medical students, himself included, to supply the corpses needed for dissection classes.

REV RICHARD SYMES (1722-1799)

The Rector of St Werburghs in Corn Street for 45 years was an evangelical clergyman in the Church of England. Richard Symes believed not only in the power of prayer, but also electricity, to cure the ailments afflicting his congregation. He bought an electrical machine for administering shocks to relevant parts of the body and kept a record of the outcomes. Symes published these case studies in a 1771 book, *Fire Analysed*, which also argued that electricity was a gift, or "divine fire", sent directly by God for the benefit of mankind.

DR JOHN TILL ADAMS (1748-1786)

He was much admired as a model medic by everyone who knew him. The young Quaker proved to be extremely versatile. John Till Adams set himself up as an apothecary and druggist, with a shop in Broad Street. He also learned the new role of man-midwife, for which he was hired at the new Bristol Dispensary, and qualified as a trained surgeon. Finally, he was awarded a medical degree by Aberdeen University to become a physician. At the same time, Till Adams experimented with electric shocks on some of his patients and friends, including Sarah Champion Fox. His blossoming career was cut short when he died of typhoid in 1786.

ANN TILL ADAMS (1752-1817)

Ann was a Fry before she and John married and ran an apothecary/druggist shop in Broad Street together. Ann proved very adept at concocting the medicines that he prescribed, and won respect for her skill in treating patients herself. Although not allowed formal medical training because she was a woman, Ann continued a successful career after her husband's death. She opened her own druggist shop in Union Street and became a rare female practitioner listed in the Matthews trade directory.

REV JOHN WESLEY (1703-1791)

The Methodist leader is famous for his charismatic preaching, but his passionate faith in electric shocks to cure illness and disease is little known. Wesley installed an electrical machine in each of his free medical dispensaries for the poor in Bristol and London. He even experimented with one to treat his own aches and pains. In a book on the subject published in 1760, *The Desideratum*, Wesley gave 49 examples of electrification allegedly resulting in a cure. He also listed about 40 ailments for which, he claimed, patients had been successfully treated.

DR BATH OF BRISTOL

The disproportionately big role played by Quakers in Bristol's industry and commerce during the eighteenth century is well documented. Less so is their major influence on the health professions and whole social fabric of the city. Often the same Quaker families who made a fortune - the Harfords, Goldneys, Champions and Frys, to name but a few - then ploughed back some of that wealth into subsidising local health and education reforms.

The businessman and amateur doctor Shurmer Bath was always there in the background, a shadowy presence but with a finger in every charity pie. I've searched in vain for a portrait, silhouette or drawing of him. This isn't surprising, as until the nineteenth century most Quakers rejected having an image of themselves created.[1]

They regarded it as an unnecessary vanity to emphasise the physical body, rather than the spirit or life within. By and large, only the wealthiest Friends of high social class commissioned portraits. A middle-ranking trader like Shurmer Bath didn't fit into this category.

However, I did come across the next best thing - a portrait of one of his two grown-up daughters, Elizabeth Bath (1774-1850), in rural Herefordshire. It was painted soon after her marriage in 1820, at the age of 48, to an Anglican clergyman, the Reverend John Jones.

He was from landed gentry and had inherited the family estate, Langstone Court near Ross-on-Wye. At the time of writing the picture still hung on a wall at the house, where descendants of the Rev. Jones still live.

Elizabeth was the daughter of Shurmer Bath and his second wife Alice, from the Dury family, who had been slave owners in Barbados. In the portrait Elizabeth is shown with one of five surviving stepchildren from the Rev. Jones's first marriage. She took on the responsibility of looking after them and spent

Portrait of Elizabeth Bath Jones with one of her stepchildren, painted by Thomas Ballard, 1822. (Image: courtesy of Rev. Richard Jones.)

Portrait of the Rev John Jones, Herefordshire clergyman, by Thomas Ballard. He married Elizabeth Bath in 1820. (Image: courtesy of Rev. Richard Jones)

the last 30 years of her life with the Jones family. Like her father, Elizabeth became known for her charitable work in the local community.

We may not know what Shurmer Bath looked like, but we do know where in Bristol he lived. The Bath family home was 93 Stokes Croft, which is still standing today. An early trade directory listed him at that address in 1775.[2] He shared the premises with his second wife Alice; their infant daughters Elizabeth and Sarah; and Shurmer's eight-year-old other daughter Mary, from his first marriage to Alice's cousin. The latter, also called Mary, had died in childbirth in 1768.[3]

At the time of writing, in 2021, number 93 Stokes Croft is an art shop you can hardly miss, called Neon Tiger. The striking coloured murals, so attractive to many of us now, wouldn't appeal to Shurmer Bath if he were still around today. Quakers of his time disapproved of exotic designs and favoured a plain look.

The Sketchley directory listed Shurmer's Quaker father-in-law, Andrew Dury (1713-1784), on the same street, living and trading as a merchant at 6 Stokes Croft. That house is long gone, swallowed up by urbanisation. Dury's family ancestors had been among the first to start planting sugar in Barbados,

93 and 95 Stokes Croft in 2021.

in the early to mid 1600s. He owned at least 60 slaves when the family sold all their estates in 1762 and relocated to Bristol.[4]

Shurmer Bath rented 93 Stokes Croft for at least six years, living there and running his business from the premises, with a malthouse out the back. In 1781 he bought the property from his landlady, Sarah Reeve, and with it the house next door, number 95. He appears to have needed financial help in the purchase from his well off younger brother Neville, who was a cutler in the Redcliffe area of the city.[5]

STOKES CROFT – A PLACE IN THE COUNTRY

The distinctive pair of gabled houses, 93 and 95, are both Grade Two Listed Buildings, dating back to the late seventeenth century. They were among the

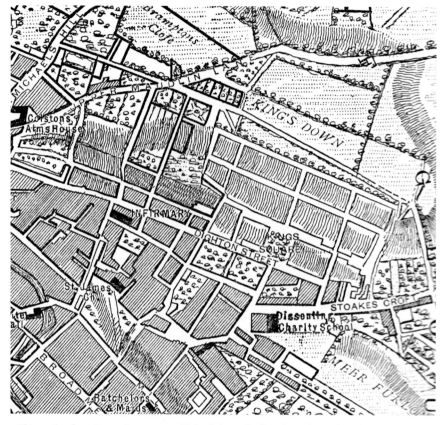

This section from Rocque's 1747 map of Bristol shows the first signs of creeping urbanisation along "Stoakes Croft", but still almost no development on "King's Down". The new Infirmary is clearly marked, as is the Dissenting Charity School for boys at Lewins Mead. The latter was founded in 1722 by a group of businessmen from the Unitarian nonconformist congregation.

first to be built on Stokes Croft, which lay at what was then the far northern edge of Bristol.[6]

The street name Stokes Croft originates from the 1300s. It was a croft, or enclosed piece of land, belonging to John Stoke, who served three times as Mayor of Bristol.

John Latimer's *Annals of Bristol in the Eighteenth Century* gives a description of the street in around 1700, from his perspective of the late 1800s: *"Stoke's Croft was a rural promenade, having fields on either side, and was sheltered from the summer sun by rows of trees."*[7]

Neighbouring Kingsdown, the hill above Stokes Croft, hadn't yet been built on and remained open countryside: *"Kingsdown was literally a down, ramblers*

Urban Stokes Croft in 2021: shabby chic, bohemian and vibrant.

on which beheld a 'grove' of church steeples on the one hand and stretches of pasture land and orchards on the other."

After Shurmer Bath died in 1800, his widow Alice lived on at 93 and/or 95 Stokes Croft until her own death in 1809.[8] Up to the age of about 16, when the Dury family sold up and sailed to Bristol, Alice had been brought up on their estates in Barbados, surrounded by slave labour.[9]

Shurmer Bath was born in Barton Street, a stone's throw from Stokes Croft. His father James Bath, born in 1707, was also a Quaker and a maltster. He had moved to the city from rural Wiltshire in 1730 to marry Sarah Alexander, daughter of a Bristol wheelwright.[10] The Bath family processed barley or other grain to produce malt for brewing beer. Shurmer, the middle one of five children, took over the business at the age of about 20, after his father died in 1758.[11]

SHURMER BATH IN LONDON

At the time of his father's death, Shurmer Bath had been living in London for the past three years as an apprentice – not to a maltster, but to a patten maker called Josiah Hoskins.[12] He was another Quaker and also Shurmer's brother-in-law, married to his older sister Elizabeth. (Pattens were wooden under-shoes for lifting you above the muddy streets.)

Shurmer must have broken the terms of his seven-year apprenticeship to return home and run the family malthouse. This was a common occurrence in the eighteenth century. In theory the indenture could only be broken by a magistrate. In practice, though, only about half of apprentices completed their full term.[13]

A career supplying malt to the brewers was almost guaranteed to give you a secure income, because people across England drank a huge amount of beer. They did so even when they were ill. For example, early records of the Bristol Infirmary show the standard diet for inpatients on the ward included *"three pints of small* [weak] *beer"* a day.[14]

Supplies of drinking water were often heavily contaminated, so people turned to beer as an alternative. Brewers needed a reliable local source of malt to satisfy demand from households, as well as from the pubs.

So, how did a boy from quite an ordinary background make himself sufficiently polished and well educated to shine on the Quaker dinner party circuit in Bristol? One can only imagine that Shurmer Bath took full advantage of new opportunities in the capital to read widely, attend public lectures and broaden his horizons, while keeping his Quaker religious fervour and moral discipline.

Life with his brother-in-law Josiah and sister Elizabeth in London was probably a bit unconventional, too. Their marriage in 1750, when she was only 19, had been officially recorded as *"clandestine"*, or without her parents' consent, because of her age. The couple were later both to die young, in their thirties, from *"consumption"* (tuberculosis).[15]

"QUAKERVILLE"

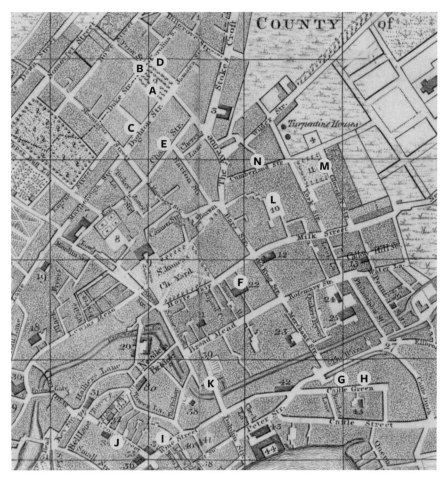

Extract from Benjamin Donne's map of Bristol, 1793 (Know Your Place)

From the mid eighteenth century a cluster of Bristol's most influential Quakers lived and worked in the congested area between Stokes Croft, on the northern edge, and the medieval city centre. It was an enclave where prosperous religious dissenters all knew each other - from doing business deals, attending the same meeting house or chapel for worship and socialising together in their homes. The Friends' Meeting House stood within easy reach at Quakers Friars. This close proximity to each other was a natural consequence of their shared identity as members of a Quaker religious community.

Each red letter superimposed on the map above represents the home of an individual who will feature in this book. In 1775 **Joseph Beck** (1721-1793), a wealthy Quaker whose family owned the Ashley Estate on Bristol's north-east fringes, had a residence at 28 King Square (red letter **A** on the map).[16] This was in addition to his family home, later known as Frenchay Manor, in countryside outside the city. Beck was a key figure in charities funding the Bristol Infirmary and new Bristol Dispensary, which both stood very close to King Square. His son-in-law, **Edward Ash** (1736-1818), who became a long-serving treasurer of the Infirmary, later moved into the same terrace at no 18 King Square (**B**). The Ash family fortune had come from manufacturing sweet raisin wine.

Joseph Harford (1741-1802), a well off banker and investor in brass and copper manufacturing, had built himself a magnificent new villa, Harford House, a stone's throw away in Dighton Street (**C**). It's still there, now providing accommodation for Bristol University students. Joseph, too, had a long spell (12 years) as Infirmary treasurer. He left the Quakers in 1780, converted to Anglicanism and became the city's Mayor in 1794. **Mark Harford** (1738-1781), a Quaker from the same banking family, lived at 2 King Square (**D**).

Prominent figures from other nonconformist religions had also staked a presence in the locality. The Methodist minister and composer of hymns, **Charles Wesley** (1707-1788) lived at 4 Charles Street (**E**) with his wife Sally and their three children.

Portrait of Charles Wesley, by John Russell.
(Image: John Wesley House & Museum of Methodism, London)

King Square

Harford House in Dighton Street,
now providing student accommodation

Charles Wesley's house at 4 Charles Street

That house has survived, too, restored inside to its original appearance. It was Charles and Sally Wesley's home from 1749. He was still listed there in 1775 by the Sketchley directory, although the family would soon move to London. His brother **John Wesley** (1703-1791) had lived part-time in accommodation at his New Room chapel in Broadmead (**F**) for much of the previous 30 years.

A short walk further on, in the central old city, you arrived at a house shared by **Richard Champion** (1743-1791) with his wife Judith and sister **Sarah Champion** (1742-1811), the diarist. This was at 17 Castle Green (**G**), next to Richard's porcelain factory making Bristol China. He was another Quaker who served as the Infirmary treasurer. The Champions' young friend **Dr Edward Long Fox** (1761-1835), who was to become famous for his humane treatment of mental illness, moved into a neighbouring house, 16 Castle Green (**H**), in 1786.[17]

8 Narrow Wine Street (**I**) was the home of **Joseph Fry** (1728-1787), the former apothecary turned chocolate manufacturer, and his wife **Anna Fry** (1732-1803). A century and a half later that whole area of the city would be devastated by bombing in the Second World War.

However, one part of the old city that would largely survive the bombs was Broad Street (**J**). There, and afterwards in nearby Union Street (**K**), a young Quaker woman, **Ann Till Adams** (1752-1817), ran a highly successful apothecary and druggist shop. Ann, whose original family name was Fry, took it over following the death of her illustrious husband **John Till Adams** (1748-1786). The couple had previously shared the business, with Ann in charge of dispensing the medicine.[18]

In 1790, when the now middle-aged diarist Sarah Champion married a banker, Charles Fox, the newly-weds moved into 14 St James Square (**L**). The square was an early Georgian gem, but also obliterated later by wartime bombing.

After her husband's death in 1801, Sarah sold that residence to an American Quaker physician, **Dr Thomas Pole** (1753-1829), and bought a smaller house in neighbouring Brunswick Square (**M**). Dr Pole was an early specialist in midwifery and obstetrics, of international renown. He also preached regularly as a Quaker minister and was a talented artist.[19]

Just off Brunswick Square, 12 Cumberland Street (**N**) was home to **Dr Abraham Ludlow** (1737-1807), a flamboyant hospital physician and surgeon.

Castle Park in 2021, with the bomb-damaged St Peter's Church left as a reminder of the Bristol Blitz. Ancient streets where the Fry and Champion families had lived were destroyed by the bombs.

Broad Street, where John and Ann Till Adams ran a druggist shop in the 1770s and 1780s.

'A View of St James Square from the South', watercolour drawing by Dr Thomas Pole, circa 1806.
(Image: courtesy of Bristol Culture, Bristol Museum & Art Gallery, K4352)

Brunswick Square, St Pauls

He also became the family doctor of choice for many local Quakers, including Sarah Champion Fox, if they could afford his fees for a house call. The well off Dr Ludlow had a second address, in Brunswick Square. He was a key figure in trying to inoculate people more safely against smallpox, 30 years before Edward Jenner succeeded with his cowpox vaccination.

The same residences, or where they once stood, can be tracked on the modern map below, if you'd like to walk the route. A key is provided to the blue numbers shown.

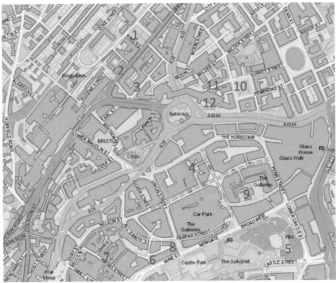

Extract from 2019 map of Bristol (Know Your Place)

1 King Square – Joseph Beck, Edward Ash, Mark Harford

2 Dighton St – Joseph Harford

3 Charles St – Charles Wesley

4 New Room, Broadmead – John Wesley

5 Castle Green - Richard and Sarah Champion (street now gone)

6 Narrow Wine St - Joseph and Anna Fry (street now gone)

7 Broad St – John and Ann Till Adams

8 Union St – Ann Till Adams

9 Quakers Friars, eighteenth century former Friends' Meeting House

10 Brunswick Square – Sarah Champion Fox (in later life), Dr Abraham Ludlow

11 Cumberland St – Dr Abraham Ludlow

12 St James Square - Sarah and Charles Fox, later Dr Thomas Pole (square now gone)

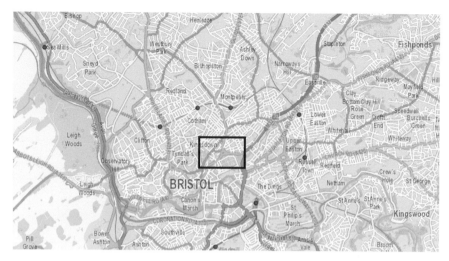

A red box, superimposed on the 2019 map of Bristol, shows the position and size of Georgian "Quakerville", as it would be in relation to the greatly expanded modern city.

It was a tight-knit community and a strong one, born out of necessity after Quakers suffered persecution, until about 1700, for rejecting the established Church. In Bristol you could be put in the stocks, brutally beaten or even imprisoned just for attending a Society of Friends meeting.[20] Quakers believe every individual has a direct personal relationship with God. They lived by a strict moral code and, as pacifists, refused to fight for their country.[21]

By the early 1700s the persecution had largely stopped, but Quakers were still blocked from some professions and from holding political office. They formed just a small minority of the population. The total number of Quakers in Bristol at the start of the eighteenth century has been estimated at well under a thousand.[22] In a city of about 20,000 that's less than five per cent.

Nevertheless, Bristol had a higher proportion of Quakers than any other English city.[23] They achieved more non-political power and influence than elsewhere by teaming up to help the most infirm and disadvantaged Bristolians. These well off dissenters took a lead role in donating and fundraising for charity across Bristol, especially when the cause was related to health or education.

From 1739 to 1778 eight consecutive treasurers of the new Bristol Infirmary were all Quakers and nearly all from the same influential family, the Champions.[24] They included Sarah's brother, the porcelain manufacturer Richard Champion. For a further three decades, from 1779 to 1808, Joseph

Harford, then Edward Ash, also served as the Infirmary treasurer.

Joseph Beck sat on the committee with them at various times. Beck was also an early president and treasurer of the Bristol Dispensary at Stokes Croft, a new type of clinic that will be explored in Chapter 8. In a healthcare system dependent on charity, the city's Quaker grandees were in pole position for at least 70 years to shape its future.

In 1793 Shurmer Bath founded the Bristol School (or "Asylum") for the Blind in Callowhill Street, where nowadays the Cabot Circus shopping centre meets St

This image of Joseph Harford is an illustration from 'A History of the Bristol Royal Infirmary', by George Munro Smith, published in 1917

Pauls.[25] It later moved to a site at the top of Park Street. Shurmer appointed the diarist Sarah Champion Fox's husband, Charles Fox, as treasurer to raise subscriptions from well off benefactors.

Bristol School ("Asylum") for the Blind at its original site in Callowhill Street. Drawing by Samuel Loxton (1857-1922). (Image: Know Your Place/Bristol Library Collections)

This postcard, based on an early engraving of the School for the Blind, shows pupils working – boys making baskets and girls spinning. On the far right a customer appears to be buying a finished basket.
(Image: courtesy of Bristol Culture, Bristol Museum & Art Gallery.)

The school trained visually impaired boys and girls for future employment. They specialised in crafts like basket and mat making, the best of which were sold to the public. It became a lasting institution in the city and finally closed in 1968. Sarah Champion Fox recorded its opening in a diary entry for 18 February 1793:

"The blind school was opened to which I paid a very pleasing visit. This useful institution was begun by Shurmer Bath...Two girls, about 14 years old, were the first pupils; there was also a little boy, and 2 more were soon added." [26]

DOCTOR BATH

Shurmer Bath was known above all, though, for his philanthropy as an amateur doctor, giving away free medication to the poorest adults and their children. He ran his own free medical practice, which was extended later to the city of Bath. Sarah Champion Fox mentions this in a diary entry in February 1798. It's her one and only criticism of her friend:

"He kept lodgings at Bath to receive patients. Many of his friends regretted that so much of his time was thus occupied, as it not only deprived them of his society but of

his watchfulness in the Church, as well as his attendance at meetings for worship." [27]

Shurmer Bath himself refers to this voluntary work as a healer of the sick in his only known piece of published writing. In 1796 he added an eight-page preface to a book of sermons by a 12-year-old girl, Charlotte Rees, from a local Quaker family of wine merchants.[28]

He writes that her *"respectable and deserving parents"* had fallen on hard times after *"losses, disappointments and treacherous connections"*. Her father, the preface continues, *"sunk under his afflictions, and left her mother with five daughters in such distress as called for the most firm reliance on divine protection."*

Shurmer tells us how, three years earlier in 1793, Charlotte's family had been *"brought under my notice by the very severe indispositions of two of the daughters."* This implies that he was called out in his role as an unofficial doctor to the family's home, or treated the two girls at his own premises.

That he dispensed medicine to the poor free of charge is confirmed by an obituary in *The Monthly Magazine*, a London publication, after his death in July 1800. It gave Shurmer Bath a glowing eulogy:

He was *"commonly called Dr Bath from his dispensing large quantities of medicine to the poor gratis. One of the principal promoters of the Bristol Asylum for the Blind, of the Schools of St James and St Paul and of other charitable institutions in the city, he was a man of a humane and benevolent disposition."* [29]

As Sarah Champion Fox reported in her Diary, Shurmer *"kept lodgings at [the city of] Bath to see patients."* Therefore, it's logical to assume that he already had somewhere in Bristol for a similar purpose. Where could that be? Two possibilities spring to mind. A clue is provided by the pair of houses, 93 and 95 Stokes Croft, which he bought in 1781. He'd previously been renting no 93 and living there with his family. Now he would own it, still as their home, and also the house next door. Shurmer may well have used number 95 as a doctor's surgery and base for his medical practice.[30]

The other plausible location was a seventeenth century house, Ashley Cottage on the outer edge of St Pauls and of the city. It was later renamed as Elm Cottage and is still there at 77 Ashley Road. The title deeds state that in February 1796 the property was *"in occupation of Shurmer Bath, maltster"*. He'd been renting it from its wealthy Quaker owner Edward Ash (treasurer of the Bristol Infirmary).[31]

It's not clear whether this arrangement applied to the cottage or just its grounds, which covered about an acre. According to a document in the deeds, from 1796 Edward Ash leased Ashley Cottage, with its outbuildings, gardens and orchards, to a local haberdasher and his wife for 10 years. Shurmer Bath was living elsewhere, on Stokes Croft. Unless he had rented Ashley Cottage as a second home, or even if he did so, there was plenty of room for a medical practice and/or a bigger malthouse.

Ashley Cottage, built in the seventeenth century, is now 77 Ashley Road.
In 1796 the property, or part of it, was occupied by Shurmer Bath.

CHAPTER 3
FRY'S HEALTHY CHOCOLATE

Sarah Champion Fox (1742-1811), from one of Bristol's most prominent Quaker families, kept a regular diary for much of her life. In it she described her daily social activities and innermost thoughts in vivid detail.

Sarah recorded meeting Shurmer Bath for the first time on 12 January 1761. She was 18 years old and he was 22. It happened in the parlour of Joseph and Anna Fry's home in Narrow Wine Street. Both had been invited there to spend the evening with the Frys and other guests.

This was Sarah's first impression of the devout, but charming and urbane, maltster:

"Here I met Shurmer Bath, a young man celebrated for the goodness of his understanding and command of temper in argument. With him I had some conversation – principally on stage entertainments, of the impropriety of which he convinced me." [32]

This encounter marked the beginning of a long friendship between them - never a romance, as far as we know - that lasted to the grave. It was based on shared values, affection and relaxed enjoyment of each other's company.

Sarah Champion Fox was a lively, clever and independent-minded woman, who preferred steady friendship and companionship to the intimacy of married love. She remained single until late middle age. Sarah was 48 when, in 1790, she married Charles Fox, a banker from Plymouth and a family friend. In this book both surnames are nearly always given for her, whether she was married or not at the time, to avoid confusing her with anyone else.

The Champions were a family of wealthy Quaker industrialists. Sarah's past relatives had been involved in founding and running the Bristol Brass Works at Baptist Mills on the River Frome, then various copper and brass works on the River Avon, from the early 1700s. [33]

Her brother, Richard Champion (1743-1791), later opened a successful but

Portrait of Richard Champion, engraved from a miniature. (Image: courtesy of Bristol Culture, Bristol Museum & Art Gallery)

short-lived porcelain factory in the city centre. It produced the exquisite Bristol China, which is now a rarity. In 1774 Richard became political agent to the Bristol Whig MP Edmund Burke, and the statesman's right-hand man, before emigrating to America a decade later.

Sarah had a privileged upbringing, except that her widowed father, Joseph Champion, went to live in London with a new wife. He left his three children behind in Bristol, to be looked after by an assortment of grandmothers and aunts. Adding to her insecurity, Sarah was often separated from her brother, until she moved in with Richard and his wife Judith in young adulthood to share their home at Castle Green.

The Diary of Sarah Fox née Champion 1745-1802 is thought to have originally filled 40 volumes. However, only a manuscript of 500 pages comprising extracts from the Diary has survived. This was assembled in 1872 by Thomas Frank, then editor of the Quaker magazine *The Friend*. It's not known what happened to the original volumes.

In 2003 the Diary extracts were published in their entirety for the first time, edited by academic historian Madge Dresser and with her excellent introduction and notes. A copy is kept at Bristol Archives, available for public viewing. The Diary can also be downloaded as an online version from Google Books.

'A view through the window into the garden, with a lady writing, at 14 St James Square' [in Bristol], was painted by Dr Thomas Pole, owner of the house. Colour drawing on paper, c. 1806. Dr Pole (1753-1829) was an American Quaker physician from Philadelphia, who moved to Bristol with his family in 1802. The young woman isn't Sarah Champion Fox, but may be one of the artist's daughters. Sarah had formerly lived in the house, which she sold to the Poles. (Image: courtesy of Bristol Culture, Bristol Museum & Art Gallery, K4353.)

JOSEPH FRY – MAN OF CHOCOLATE

Silhouette of Joseph Fry (Image: courtesy of Bristol Culture, Bristol Museum & Art Gallery, J5690)

The year Shurmer Bath first met Sarah Champion Fox in Joseph Fry's parlour, 1761, was also a pivotal one for the latter. Joseph Fry (1728-1787) had recently started making chocolate and cocoa on these larger premises at 8 Narrow Wine Street, after moving there from his original apothecary's shop in nearby Small Street. He was about to acquire the patent for a water-powered machine that could grind cocoa flakes to a powder, for a smoother chocolate drink. The method had been invented by another Bristol apothecary, Walter Churchman.

Before setting up in Bristol, Joseph Fry was apprenticed to Dr Henry Portsmouth, a much-respected family doctor and druggist at Basingstoke in Hampshire. There he received extensive training in the medical properties of plants and herbs and the compounding of drugs.[34] His apprenticeship convinced Joseph that chocolate and cocoa were nutritious and beneficial to your health. It also introduced him to Dr Portsmouth's eldest daughter, Anna. They fell in love and married in 1755.

Anna Fry (1732-1803) would eventually take over the business, after Joseph's sudden death in 1787. By then production had transferred to a new purpose-built factory in neighbouring Union Street. When she handed over to their son, John Storrs Fry (1769-1835), around the turn of the century, he continued to advertise chocolate as a health-improving product. J.S. Fry and Sons would create the world's first chocolate bar in the mid 1800s, to seal the family's place in history and make it a household name.[35]

PATENT COCOA,

G E N U I N E and *UNADULTERATED,*

Made by A N N A   F R Y and S O N,

PATENTEES of *CHURCHMAN*'s CHOCOLATE,

B   R   I   S   T   O   L.

T HIS Cocoa is recommended by the moſt eminent of the Faculty, in Preference to every other Kind of Breakfaſt, to ſuch who have tender Habits, decayed Health, weak Lungs, or ſcorbutic Tendencies, being eaſy of Digeſtion, affording a fine and light Nouriſhment, and greatly correcting the ſharp Humours in the Conſtitution.

To make C O C O A in the P O T.

Take an Ounce of Cocoa (which is about a common Tea Cupful) boil it in a Pint and a Half of Water for Ten or Fifteen Minutes, then keep it near the Fire to ſettle and become fine, after that, decant it off into another Pot for *immediate* Uſe.—It is drank as Coffee, ſweetened with a fine moiſt Sugar, and a little Cream or Milk ſhould be added.

It is beſt not to be made long before it be drank, left by that Means it loſe Part of its fine Flavour.

N. B. This Cocoa does not require much Boiling; therefore it will go quite as far as any other Sort, with a leſs Quantity of Water than is commonly directed.

A late eighteenth century advertisement for Fry's Cocoa, claiming it had health benefits. This was a handbill produced by Anna Fry after she took over the business from her late husband Joseph in 1787.
(Image: John Johnson Collection, Bodleian Library, Oxford.)

AT HOME WITH THE FRYS

When Joseph Fry first began to make chocolate, working from home was the norm. For him and Anna and many other prosperous Quaker families, their business, social and religious lives merged seamlessly together. Joseph was an affable and hospitable man. The couple welcomed guests to 8 Narrow Wine Street, where they hosted supper parties and other social gatherings on a regular basis.

In contrast to Shurmer Bath, at least one image of Joseph Fry was created for posterity. These may well include the painting below, but the sitter's identity has never been confirmed. However, there's no doubt that a silhouette of a

'Portrait of a Man, said to be Joseph Fry',
British School & John Ferneley, 1816 (Image: courtesy
of Bristol Culture, Bristol Museum & Art Gallery, K6328)

Miniature of Anna Fry, circa 1781
(Image: Fry Family Tree on Ancestry website)

man in later life, and looking very similar, is him. (See the image on page 40.)

The late David Fry, a descendant who researched the definitive Fry Family Tree, wrote this of Joseph:

"He was a very clever man – kind, hospitable and generous. He had a good deal of humour and enjoyed a droll story...He had a very original mind and was very unconventional in thought and action."[36]

Sarah Champion Fox had known Joseph since she was a child. Their family ties grew when he briefly gave her brother Richard some financial help with setting up his porcelain works at Castle Green. Sarah's diary is packed with entries about visits to *"J.Fry's"*, where she *"drank tea"*, dined, supped or just spent time with him and/or Anna, either alone or in a Quaker social group.

For 23 April 1761, the Diary records: *"The many acts of kindness received from Anna Fry produced an intimacy, and are remembered with gratitude and regard."*[37]

Sarah confides in another entry that to her mind the Frys had an ideal married relationship. She wrote this when aged 18:

"Joseph and Anna Fry were one of the few couples that appeared to me to enjoy real happiness in married life – the result of a long, steady, affectionate attachment

A demonstration of animal magnetism, or mesmerism, in a French engraving, circa 1780. The woman on the far left appears to be under hypnosis, a term not used until the 1800s. (Image: HistoryofInformation.com)

that took deep root in very early life."[38]

Anna comes across in the Diary as a cheerful and humorous woman, with a spirited intelligence. Some of her practical good sense is evident, too, in a miniature of her from 1781, when she was about 50.

Diary entries by Sarah at the time of Joseph Fry's death are especially moving. On 3 April 1787 she describes him taking a lively interest in one of the latest medical science experiments.

During a trip to London Joseph had apparently been introduced to animal magnetism. This was the name given by a Viennese doctor, Franz Mesmer (1734-1815), for what he believed to be a natural force possessed by all living things. He claimed it had healing power. However, the hands-on contact that was, apparently, necessary seems very often to have been by men on attractive young females. It was a forerunner of hypnosis, which developed as a therapy from the 1820s onwards.

Animal magnetism, otherwise known as mesmerism, was more a performance for entertainment than a healing experience. It bore similarities to another eighteenth century craze, for demonstrating the effects of human contact with electricity. That much bigger phenomenon, and its influence on healthcare in Bristol, will be explored in Chapter 6.

In her diary entry for 3 April 1787, Sarah Champion Fox reported: *"After the morning meeting [for worship]... I joined Joseph Fry...& accompanied him to Fry's in B. square [Brunswick Square], where I heard a wonderful account of animal magnetism; of which, as I know nothing, I shall only say it was a subject that had much engaged his attention in London, from whence he was lately returned, & great was the demand for his company & conversation."* [39]

A fortnight later, on 16 April, Sarah refers to the chocolate manufacturer again: *"On my return from Corn Street, I found Joseph Fry at home, who staid [sic] the evening. He was very agreeable and entertaining."* [40]

A further two weeks on, Sarah received this shocking news: *"I heard the affecting and unexpected tidings of Joseph Fry's death.*

"On the next morning I wrote to his afflicted widow, & after dining in Corn Street, paid her a visit. She was in great grief, though appearing calm & acquiescent. It was some comfort to me that I was able to weep with her, as I had a sincere regard for her & her much loved deceased husband whom I had known since I was ten years old – whose useful benevolence produced universal regret at his loss, which was lamented in an uncommon manner by his acquaintance as well as his Friends." [41]

The diarist joined many other mourners for Joseph Fry's funeral at the Quakers Friars burial ground: *"The procession was large and the house crowded."* [42]

Around this time a new Quaker physician at the Bristol Infirmary, Dr Edward Long Fox, tried out animal magnetism on some of his patients. It was hypnosis in all but name. He wanted to know whether mesmerism had the power to heal, as its practitioners claimed. [43]

However, Mesmer was regarded by many in Britain as a quack. In 1789 Dr Fox's experimental treatment brought a hostile reaction from some of his colleagues and he came under attack in the local press. His efforts allegedly *"threw some Patients at the Infirmary into a Crisis, whether pretended, or real, or the mere effect of Terror"*. [44]

Dr Fox eventually gave up on animal magnetism, saying he'd found no evidence of any beneficial effect. We'll return to Fox, and his key later work as a psychiatrist, in Chapter 11.

THE SHURMERS AND FRYS OF WILTSHIRE

Shurmer Bath and Joseph Fry had a lot in common and were kindred spirits in many ways. Both were amiable, sociable and clever men, with a shared interest in medicine and strong Quaker belief in discipline and good behaviour towards others.

In one Diary entry, for 5 February 1788, Sarah Champion Fox recalled an after-dinner discussion between Shurmer and other guests, which became rather heated. There were five men at the table, all Quakers, and she made this observation:

"Such a collection could not fail of producing interesting conversation. In the course of it, opportunities occurred of remarking that, however dignified by understanding or enobled by religion, every man retains his favourite sentiment which becomes so much his hobby horse as, if he has not command of temper, will make him apt to quarrel with those not willing to ride it...Shurmer seemed willing to let all ride quietly in their own way." [45]

Shurmer Bath, his father-in-law Andrew Dury and Joseph Fry were all long-serving members of the Bristol Quaker Men's Meeting. This was an all-male committee which dealt with disciplinary matters and oversaw the Monthly Meeting. The latter was open to both men and women and conducted most of the Society of Friends' local business. [46]

The Morning and Evening Meetings were for worship, often with a minister speaking and with an elder in charge. Elders, appointed by the congregation, had a responsibility for their spiritual welfare. Ministers preached, but were lay people and not ordained clergy. Andrew Dury (1713-1784), the former slave owner now part of Shurmer's family, became a minister, then an elder, late in life in Bristol. He'd previously been a leading member of the Quaker religious community in Barbados.

Often a guest minister - sometimes a visitor from America passing through - was invited to speak at a Meeting. The Friends in Bristol had close ties with their transatlantic counterparts. A few ministers were women, including Sarah Champion Fox herself. Her close personal friend Catherine Philips travelled extensively in Britain and America as an itinerant preacher. [47]

It was a bureaucratic system but also a great leveller. The Quakers kept

Death certificates of Andrew Dury, signed by Joseph Fry, and of Fry himself. (Images: Quaker Records)

Chocolate Cup, British Museum, circa 1775, made at Richard Champion's Bristol China works.

meticulous and detailed records of their births, marriages and deaths. All were expected to do their bit. For example, when Andrew Dury died in 1784, it was Joseph Fry who signed his death certificate as register to the Bristol Monthly Meeting. Three years later another Friend did the same for Joseph on his death. In the 1770s Shurmer Bath took his turn in a similar registration role.

The Bath and Fry families both had Quaker roots in the same part of north Wiltshire. Shurmer's father, James Bath, was born in Purton Stoke and Joseph Fry in Sutton Benger, villages just a few miles apart on either side of Malmesbury. Shurmer was a local surname on his mother's side, dating back to at least the sixteenth century. It was commonplace for Quakers to use both their parents' family names. In the maltster's case his parents made Shurmer his first name.

One ancestor, Margaret Shurmer (1645-1710), was a prosperous widow and mother whose home in Purton served as the Quakers' local Meeting House during her final years. She took charge of the Purton Particular Meeting (for worship), which at the time had 37 women members and 48 men. As its leader - exceptional for a woman - Margaret also acted as an important mediator in internal disputes.[48]

The Fry links with Wiltshire may originate from the arrival of religious refugees from continental Europe in the sixteenth and seventeenth centuries.

Many were textile workers. They settled in towns like Trowbridge, Chippenham and Bradford-on-Avon, which were centres of the Wiltshire clothing trade. Quakerism also flourished in the same areas.[49]

The Fry family had a myriad of branches in Wiltshire and Bristol. In 1729 Christian Fry, daughter of a clothier, Henry Fry, from Calstone Wellington near Calne, married John Shurmer. He was a *"mealman"* (grain merchant) from Devizes.

Among guests at the ceremony in Calne, listed in the Quaker Records as a relative, was our Shurmer's father, James Bath. James's own mother was a Shurmer, and she'd married a Bath. To some degree, therefore, all three families became interrelated well before the first cup of Fry's chocolate was poured in Bristol.

CHAPTER 4

SHURMER BATH'S RESTORATIVE PILLS

As soon as Shurmer Bath was *"removed"* in 1800 - to quote an expression for death repeatedly used in Sarah Champion Fox's Diary - an astonishing development followed. Members of his family shamelessly exploited his name to launch *"Shurmer Bath's Restorative or Strengthening Pills"* as a commercial product.

The tablets he'd always supplied free to hard up patients were now to be sold for profit, by the boxful, in the shops. During the summer of 1802 a lengthy and detailed advertisement was placed in all the London newspapers.[50]

It claimed the pills were an effective treatment for a long list of conditions, mainly stomach-related and afflicting young females in particular. They were stocked in several chemist shops and other outlets in fashionable parts of the capital, as well as in Bristol and other towns.

The advert is worth reproducing in full to show the extent of its highly ambitious claims. Since the text is not always fully legible, a transcript has been added.

Grand announcements in the press about unbelievably effective drugs were all too common. Shurmer Bath must have been turning in his grave, at the Quaker burial ground in Redcliffe, after the family's decision to charge for his pills. But did they work and were they worth buying?

A pill that relieves indigestion, wind and flatulence in pallid girls who indulge in an overactive social life, and refuse to take exercise, sounds a bit too good to be true. A pill that will also treat *"Bilious or Hysterical complaints"*, headaches and jaundice, and cure whooping cough and rickets, seems nothing short of miraculous!

The only other advertisement I came across for Shurmer Bath's pills was a much shorter version, published 16 years later in 1818, and this time in a

BATH's RESTORATIVE,
OR STRENGTHENING PILLS.
TO THE PUBLIC.

MANY of the Friends of the late SHURMER BATH, of Briftol, who were witneffes of the powerful effects of his Reftorative or Strengthening Pills, are defirous fo beneficial a Medicine fhould be made known to the world. During many years extenfive practice, the Proprietor forbore to give them publicity, and fcrupuloufly avoided pecuniary advantage to himfelf or family; yet their merit is fo well known in the city and neighbourhood where he refided, that that there are few of the inhabitants who would not give teftimony to their excellence.

They are particularly ufeful in all complaints to which Females are fubject, and are peculiarly adapted to the conftitution of Girls of about twelve or thirteen years of age; and for thofe young Women who have pallid complexions, are afflicted with fhortnefs of breath, and great reluctance to exercife, thefe pills are a fpecific; as they, in a fhort time, reftore to the Blood its loft Craffamentum, and thereby give the bloom of Health to the paleft cheek.

They are a remedy for all difeafes that originate in the Stomach; the loft tone of which they fpeedily reftore; they remove Flatulencies, expel wind, create an Appetite, and promote Digeftion. They have been found extremely efficacious in Bilious and Hyfterical complaints, Pains in the Head, Jaundice, and in broken and decayed Conftitutions, from free living or a variety of other caufes. They have been repeatedly known to cure the Hooping Cough; and when given to Weakly or Ricketty Children, they rarely fail effecting a cure.

They are carefully prepared by the Family, and fold wholefale and retail by Bailer and Howell, Wine-ftreet, Briftol; alfo in London, wholefale and retail, by F. Smith, Druggift, Haymarket; and retail by Darton and Harvey, Gracechurch-ftreet; and William Clark, Confectioner, in the Borough; in Boxes

Advertisement in the Star (London) newspaper on 14 July 1802. (Image: British Newspaper Archive)

BATH'S RESTORATIVE
OR STRENGTHENING PILLS
TO THE PUBLIC

MANY of the Friends of the late SHURMER BATH, of Bristol, who were witnesses of the powerful effects of his Restorative or Strengthening Pills, are desirous so beneficial a Medicine should be made known to the world. During many years extensive practice, the Proprietor forebore to give them publicity and scrupulously avoided pecuniary advantage to himself or family; yet their merit is so well known in the city and neighbourhood where he resided that there are few of the inhabitants who would not give testimony to their excellence.

They are particularly useful in all complaints to which Females are subject, and are peculiarly adapted to the constitutions of Girls of about twelve or thirteen years of age; and for those young women who have pallid complexions, are afflicted with shortness of breath, and great reluctance to exercise, these pills are a specific; as they, in a short time, restore to the blood its lost momentum, and thereby give the bloom of Health to the palest cheek.

They are a remedy for all diseases that originate in the Stomach; the lost tune of which they speedily restore; they remove Flatulencies, expel wind, create an Appetite, and promote Digestion. They have been found extremely efficacious in Bilious and Hysterical complaints, Pains in the Head, Jaundice, and in broken and decayed Constitutions, from free living or a variety of other causes. They have been repeatedly known to cure the Hooping Cough; and when given to Weakly or Rickety children, they rarely fail effecting a cure.

They are carefully prepared by the Family, and sold wholesale and retail by Baller and Howell, Wine-street, Bristol; also in London, wholesale and retail, by F.Smith, Druggist, Haymarket; and retail by Dawson and Harvey. Gracechurch-street; and William Clark, Confectioner, in the Borough. In boxes at 1s 6d, 2s 6d, 4s.

provincial newspaper.

The period in between was dominated by the Napoleonic Wars with France, when the nation's attention and resources were focused on the war effort. Therefore, the circumstances for launching a new product unconnected with the French threat were far from ideal. It may explain the long gap, since 1802, before this notice in the Salisbury and Winchester Journal:

PRINTING-OFFICE, SALISBURY, *Jan*. 31, 1818.

MESSRS. BRODIE and DOWDING have just received from Bristol a fresh Supply of the late SHURMER BATH'S RESTORATIVE PILLS, which have been for many years justly celebrated for their efficacy in the Restoration of Health to Females, and in relieving obstruction in stomachic plenitude, or too great a redundancy of bile. These Pills will be found a sovereign remedy for all diseases that originate in the stomach, the lost tone of which they speedily restore.—Sold in boxes at 1s. 6d. and 2s. 6d. each, accompanied with ample directions. [3358

Salisbury & Winchester Journal, 2 February 1818 (Image: British Newspaper Archive)

The earlier advertising blitz for the *"late Shurmer Bath's Restorative Pills"* raises a couple of obvious questions:

Who in the family placed the ads and *"carefully prepared"* the pills for sale? Why did they seek *"pecuniary advantage"* from the pills, although Shurmer never had?

The second question is easily answered. Shurmer Bath's widow Alice and daughters Mary and Elizabeth were heavily in debt, inherited from his failed investment in building houses.[51]

It's a logical assumption that they began selling his pills for profit in order to raise the money owed.

As for how and where the pills were manufactured, and by whom, we should first take a look at the wider picture – the state of medicine in Bristol in the mid to late 1700s.

CHAPTER 5

DESPERATE REMEDIES

For much of the eighteenth century literally anyone could call themselves a doctor and set up a medical practice, with no qualifications and little or no training. Healthcare went largely unregulated. Many doctors in Bristol were competent professionals, but standards varied enormously. There were also practitioners who overcharged their patients for ineffective treatment they couldn't afford.

Shurmer Bath fell into a different category, that of amateur medics with limited knowledge but good intentions. Their motive was philanthropic - to help the poorest among the sick.

William Dyer (1730-1801) was a friend of Shurmer's who also took up medicine as an amateur sideline. He felt a close affinity with Quakers and shared their moral outlook, but remained in the Anglican Church. Dyer made a comfortable living as a clerk for a gunpowder works and as a freelance accountant. In his spare time he prescribed medicine to a list of sick patients, unpaid, or treated them with electrical therapy. At the age of 14 William Dyer had been apprenticed to an apothecary (part GP, part chemist), but left after only a few months.[52]

Unlike Shurmer Bath, Dyer left a written account of his activities. He kept a detailed Diary from 1751 to 1801, but destroyed most of the original volumes. Only his Diary for 1762 and extracts from others have survived.

During 1762 William recorded prescribing and preparing concoctions with ingredients that included bark, Balm of Gilead, quicksilver, elderflower, marshmallow and hemlock. All of them corresponded to remedies used by professional medics.[53]

There was a long tradition in England of ordinary people making their own medicines, from the plants and herbs growing wild or in their gardens. As part of everyday conversation, they exchanged ideas with their friends and neighbours on which ingredients might work best for a particular ailment.

Some of these recommendations came from popular health texts, like the seventeenth century *The English Physician Enlarged* by Nicholas Culpeper. These sought to demystify medicine for the common man or woman. However, by William Dyer's time such remedy books relied increasingly on commercial products, which were often very expensive.[54]

Dyer planted hemlock in his garden and made pills from it himself. But his most frequent standby was Dr James's Fever Powder. This was patented by a *bona fide* London physician, Dr Robert James, in 1746. The main ingredients, kept secret by its creator, were antimony and calcium phosphate.[55]

Despite a lack of evidence on its efficacy, the powder quickly became a standard remedy, accepted by the medical establishment. In the 1760s, it was claimed, shops sold nationally over 80,000 doses a year. But the fever powder cost two and a half shillings a packet, which could amount to half a week's wages for the average labourer.[56]

William Dyer frankly admitted the fever powder didn't always work, in a Diary entry for 17 May 1762:

"Rose this morning about 7 & was greatly shocked when I went into town, on being informed that poor Mr Giles expired last night about 9 o'clock. When I was there at 5 o'clock the same evening I advis'd 'em to Dr James's powders which they procured but declined administering 'em until Dr Drummond came, when he approv'd of it & half a paper was given but it prov'd ineffectual, as he expired soon after & left a very disconsolate wife with 8 children behind him. He was sensible to ye very last. He sent for a lawyer to make his will & had given instructions but before the attorney cou'd finish writing the same poor Giles was no more to this world. May the Lord prepare me for so awful a change."[57]

William really cared about his patients, as the Diary repeatedly makes clear. On 25 October he visited *"poor Miss Roe"*, a young woman who lay gravely ill with paralysed hands and feet.[58]

He *"advised make a decoction of marshmallow & elder flowers & stupe her reins & abdomen...pills 1 to be taken at 11 another this eve & ye other tomor morn provided she does not make water."*

The next day, William's Diary tells us, he awoke from a bad dream, in which he found Miss Roe dying in agonising pain. Her death followed in reality a

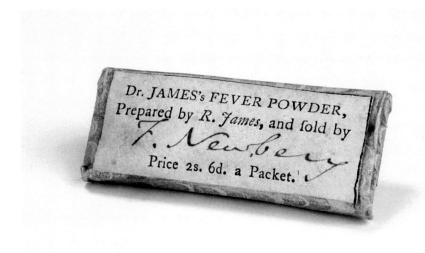

An original and unopened packet of Dr James's Fever Powder, circa 1770.
(Image: History of Science Museum, Oxford)

short time later, much to his distress and worry that he was to blame.

"I was greatly alarmed at my dream, lest ye pills I had left yesterday had proved of any bad consequence – but I find she only took one of 'em & no kind of operation perceived."

The risky attempts by William Dyer, Shurmer Bath and other practitioners in Bristol to treat their patients with electricity will be explored in the next chapter.

BRISTOL APOTHECARIES AND SURGEONS

In the 1700s a large majority of professional practitioners in Bristol were classed as apothecaries or surgeons. Apothecaries had a jack-of-all-trades medical role. They combined general practice as a family doctor with prescribing and dispensing medicine, plus a bit of surgery and even midwifery when required.

Their versatility paid dividends. Throughout the eighteenth century apothecaries held their own in fierce competition with the surgeons, who also had to be flexible to meet the demands of their patients.

By 1793 Bristol found itself awash with a diverse variety of practitioners. That year the city had a total of 35 apothecaries, still outnumbered by about

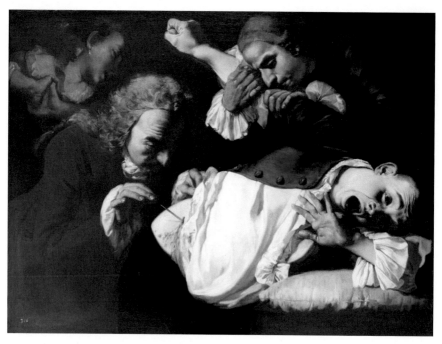

Surgery in the mid 1700s: 'The Operation (the Wound)' by an Italian painter, Gaspare Traversi, circa 1753.
(With the Matthiesen Gallery 1989. Photo: Matthiesen Ltd)

50 surgeons, In addition, a dozen barber-surgeons hung on in their traditional role, setting bones or bleeding patients, as well as shaving them and cutting their hair. But they were gradually being replaced by a new wave of hospital-trained surgeons.[59]

Physicians - senior doctors with a university degree - formed a small minority of the medical workforce, as did trained druggists. The latter were forerunners of the modern pharmacist. In the late eighteenth century druggists started to rival apothecaries, by offering better medication at lower prices, and were rapidly moving up the scale.

Matthews' New Bristol Directory for the Year 1793-4 listed practitioners from all the main categories in its *"Physic."* section. The list came to a grand total of 82 names, which was definitely an underestimate. It left out their apprentices and the unofficial amateurs like Shurmer Bath and William Dyer, of whom there were an unknown number. In a rapidly expanding population, by then of 70,000, it's clear the city had more than enough healthcare providers, although sometimes of very dubious quality.

Young apothecaries received training via a seven-year apprenticeship to another apothecary. They could then charge the public whatever fee they liked, but only for dispensing medicine, not for a doctor's consultation. This led to them massively overprescribing - and their patients being routinely overcharged as a result.

Some extraordinary examples have been passed down to us, from over 200 years ago, by a contemporary who saw or heard it all. Richard Smith junior (1772-1843) eventually became an eminent and long-serving surgeon at the Bristol Infirmary. But he started

Portrait of Richard Smith junior, surgeon at the Bristol Infirmary, by John Hazlitt, 1824. (Image: Wellcome Library. Reproduced under Creative Commons Attribution only licence *CC* BY 4.0)

off his career as the apprentice of a local apothecary.

The dividing lines between an apothecary, a surgeon and a druggist were far more blurred in those days than between the various types of practitioner we have now. Nearly all the Bristol surgeons also dispensed medicine, as well as mending fractures and dressing wounds, because it was so lucrative. Richard Smith cites his own experience as an example, when he set up a practice in College Street. His door plate at the front read "Smith, Surgeon", while on the back door in Lamb Street was written: "Smith, Surgeon and Apothecary."[60]

His apprenticeship had been with a notorious character by the name of William Broderip. Smith later included him in his biographical memoirs. These are now held by Bristol Archives in 14 volumes, which are as entertaining as they are jaw-dropping. Many of his same recollections are also found in the book *A History of the Bristol Royal Infirmary*. This was compiled by a surgeon of the early twentieth century, George Munro Smith, and first published in 1917.

BILLY BRODERIP

William Broderip (1747-1826) became a partner in a highly successful apothecary practice in the upmarket Queen Square, Bristol, in 1775. By the end of the century he was earning up to £5,000 a year. That would be about three-quarters of a million in today's money. Broderip, known to associates as "Billy", got seriously rich by prescribing and dispensing far more doses than his patients needed.[61] He was perhaps the worst culprit, but not the only one.

Richard Smith writes: *"In fact, the amount of medicines consumed in those days is almost incredible. Patients with ordinary maladies not unfrequently paid the apothecary a guinea a day for their drugs, and scores of packets containing "the draught", "the julep", and "the powders as before" were never untied, and cupboards were loaded with hundreds of bottles, empty and full."*

He tells us most of them had no effect, the potions consisting largely of elm bark and almond emulsion and the powders made from rhubarb and chalk. For a packet of 12 powder doses you paid four shillings - the equivalent of about £30 in modern terms.

Smith also describes some weird and wonderful prescriptions used at the Infirmary in the eighteenth century. They're reminiscent of the witches' brew in *Macbeth*:

"Goat's blood dried in the sun or by a slow fire, bees shut up in a clean vessel and dried at a slow heat, and powdered toads were used. The latter were prepared...as follows: Take live toads, dip them in oil of soot – then let them be burned in a pot at a moderate heat and pulverise them".

Although Broderip made no charge for house calls in the city, he demanded five shillings (worth around £40 today) for a visit beyond its boundaries, to Stapleton, Brislington or Redland. One out-of-town couple rated his medicines so highly that they bulk purchased every year 200 draughts of tonic and 1,000 pills. A patient in Portland Square, St Pauls, swallowed a dozen draughts daily, costing him 18 shillings (equivalent to £130 now).

Hard-pressed assistants were kept busy from morning to midnight preparing the medicines. Richard Smith recalls: *"There were no pill-making machines in those days; the mass was rolled out into a long, worm-like piece and divided into the requisite number of fragments, each of which was rolled into a pill. No wonder that one of Broderip's assistants declared he was sick to death with rolling them."*

Broderip's lifestyle reflected his wealth. He kept a coach and horses and employed a coachman for making up to 60 house calls a day. He bought some land between Durdham Down and Westbury-on-Trym to have a large country house built, with grounds allegedly designed by the landscaper Humphry Repton.[62] The Broderip family moved into Cote Bank, their new home, and entertained there regularly, surrounded by fine furnishings and art works. Locals maliciously named it "Gallipot Hall". (Gallipots were small jars for medicine.)

However, Billy Broderip was heading for a fall. He started drinking heavily at home and the alcohol *"made him moody, touchy and averse to business."* In fact, as the nineteenth century began, the age of the apothecary was almost over. They had been supplanted by rivals offering a better and cheaper service – the dispensing druggists. Broderip sold up in 1815 and went to live quietly in Richmond Terrace, Clifton, for the final decade of his life.

According to Smith's reminiscences, Broderip still kept up a small practice, but *"never held up his head again. If you chanced to pass him on the street, he hurried by you under a confused salute, and it was pitiful in the extreme to all those who had known him and partaken of his hospitality when fortune smiled upon him."*

Cote Bank, the mansion near Westbury-on-Trym where Broderip had lived in his pomp, was demolished in the 1930s, to make way for new houses built alongside Falcondale Road.

HUSBAND AND WIFE MEDICAL TEAM

A brilliant young medic, John Till Adams, and his equally talented wife Ann were a key factor in bringing druggists to the fore in Bristol. The couple were both Quakers and part of the diarist Sarah Champion Fox's inner social circle. John Till Adams (1748-1786) was the son of William Till Adams (sometimes written as Tilladams), a local shoemaker.[63] He qualified as a physician in 1780 by gaining a medical degree from Aberdeen University. John had previously trained as a druggist, apothecary, surgeon and man-midwife during his apprenticeship to Thomas Benwell, a Quaker family doctor at Whitchurch in Hampshire.

Silhouette of John Till Adams from the frontispiece of an elegy to him by a friend and fellow astrologer, Ebenezer Sibly, published after John's death in 1786.

He became a highly regarded all-rounder. The shoemaker's son was also exceptional among physicians in that his fee varied according to what the patient could afford, even reducing to zero for the poorest.[64]

John Till Adams found time for a trip to stay with American missionary Quakers in Philadelphia, before returning to Bristol and marrying Ann Fry in 1777. She was the youngest daughter of a prosperous grocer, William Fry. The married couple - both of them together - ran an apothecary and druggist shop in Broad Street, which was also their home. They shared duties, with John working out the prescriptions and choosing their ingredients, while Ann (1752-1817) made up and dispensed them.

However, John fell victim to typhoid and died in February 1786, at the age of only 37. Ann inherited his medicines and recipes for preparing them. She took over the business and moved into a shop at the top of Union Street, next to the new Fry's chocolate factory. The widow was so competent and successful that Bristol trade directories began listing Ann Till Adams as a druggist in her own right. She was one of just two women among 82 medical practitioners named in the *"Physic"* section of the Matthews directory for 1793.

Ann had picked up more than just her late husband's knowledge of making and dispensing drugs. She proved adept at treating patients herself. According to Richard Smith's memoirs, she *"obtained a reputation for cure of certain diseases"*.[65] Sarah Champion Fox wrote in her Diary of an earlier occasion, in November 1777. Sarah's friend Sally Young *"had a dreadful putrid fever, from which she recovered by means of the skill & attention of Dr Ludlow & A. Till Adams"*.[66]

This episode took place only a few weeks after Ann's marriage to John Till Adams, when she was 25. Dr Abraham Ludlow, a Quaker who will loom large in this narrative in other contexts, was one of the city's most prominent physicians. However, the young woman's medical abilities shone out, even

Fry's chemists and druggists in Union Street, circa 1825. (Image: Know Your Place/Bristol Library Collections)

alongside this senior doctor.

Ann's own career in medicine, and the recognition she gained for it, was a rare achievement for any eighteenth century woman, especially a religious dissenter. Because of her sex, she was barred from the opportunities for medical training and qualifications seized by her husband.

Until the mid 1700s it was not unusual for wives to help out in a medical practice, surgery or shop, or even take over the business when necessary. By the 1770s, when the Till Adams partnership came on the scene, formal training had become more widely available, but only for men. It was now even harder for a female to win acceptance as a skilled practitioner. Yet Ann pulled it off.[67]

She belonged to a separate branch of the Fry family from the chocolate makers Joseph and Anna. Her brother John Plant Fry was a druggist, too. He took charge of their father William's grocery shop in Dolphin Street after William died in 1776. John P. Fry then married Hannah Dury, sister of Alice Dury. Alice's husband was Shurmer Bath.

Hannah and John P.'s son, another William Fry, took over the druggist shop in Union Street from his aunt, Ann Till Adams, around the turn of the century.

The same shop circa 1840, now by royal appointment to Queen Victoria. By that time the Fry name had disappeared from its sign, replaced by a new partnership of Ferris, Brown and Score.
(Image: Know Your Place/Bristol Library Collections)

The shop became a fixture there for the next hundred years. William died in 1812, aged only 33. He was replaced by his apprentice James Gibbs, who then appointed Richard Ferris as a partner in the firm.[68]

SHURMER BATH'S RESTORATIVE PILLS – SLIGHT RETURN

So, we've come full circle since the end of Chapter 4. We may now be in a better position to work out where *"Shurmer Bath's Restorative Pills"* could have been manufactured and by whom. The philanthropic "Dr Bath" offered his pills free to the poor, but his family started charging for them after his death in 1800.

It's possible that originally Shurmer made up his own remedies. His fellow amateur doctor William Dyer did this, albeit with some experience as an apothecary's apprentice, which his friend lacked. As a maltster with an interest in medicine, Shurmer perhaps knew about the health benefits of malt extract. This is the residue left from the malting process, which contains essential vitamins and minerals.

The extract was used as a dietary supplement in the early twentieth century, and for post-war malnourished children in the 1940s and 1950s.

In the modern world malt extract has also been shown to lower cholesterol, so reducing the risk of heart disease. It's still available nowadays from health food shops.[69]

The most likely candidates for making Shurmer Bath's pills were: John Till Adams (until his death in 1786); John's widow Ann (a Fry and sister-in-law of Shurmer's wife Alice); John Plant Fry (Alice's brother-in-law); the young William Fry (her nephew); or a combination of some or all of them. William Fry was chosen as an executor for Alice's will, so those two clearly had a bond.[70]

A post-war advertisement for Virol. This was a sweet and sticky mixture of malt extract and bone marrow, which commonly used to be given by the spoonful to children at school in the 1940s.

All four were trained druggists, in a Quaker family and community which believed in helping each other. Alice Bath's in-laws among the Frys would surely have rallied to her aid after Shurmer's death. They could also have made his pills during his lifetime, when Shurmer was giving them away free. These Frys had the professional know-how to manufacture and sell them as a commercial product, when a lot of cash was needed fast to pay off the Bath family debts.

However, we're in the realm of informed speculation here. These are plausible theories, but no more than that. The evidence is circumstantial and could be wide of the mark. What's certain, though, is that whether or not Shurmer Bath manufactured his own pills in his lifetime, someone else did it for profit after his death.

CHAPTER 6

BRIGHT SPARKS

By the 1750s there was widespread interest in experimenting with electricity, as an alternative to drugs, to treat patients and cure their maladies. It soon caught on in Bristol to combat a range of physical ailments, from toothache, rheumatism and strains to gout and palsy.

John Till Adams, the progressive young doctor and druggist, was fully plugged in to using electrical therapy on some of his patients. He kept one of the new electrical machines at home in Broad Street, devised for the purpose. Once again we have Sarah Champion Fox's Diary to thank for passing on this fascinating anecdote, in an entry during February 1779. Sarah had been invited to dine, with others, *"at J.T.A's"* in Broad Street.

She continues: ..."*the subject of electricity being introduced, I was prevailed with to join in receiving a shock, from the effects of which I did not recover for many hours."* [71]

We aren't told what malady the electric shock was targeting, although in later years Sarah complained of serious discomfort from rheumatism. She trusted Till Adams enough to give his machine a go, but clearly found the experience very unpleasant.

The vogue started in America with Benjamin Franklin, the great scientist, inventor and political philosopher. In 1748 Franklin created an early form of battery, which powered his "electric bath". A patient was "bathed", not in water but in electricity. This was designed to build up a high-voltage charge in his or her insulated body when connected to it. [72]

To prove his battery worked and gain some publicity, Franklin pulled off a humorous stunt. He deliberately killed several turkeys with electric shocks, roasted them on an electric spit and served them to dinner party guests. The American hoped his machine would ease pain and restore movement to paralysed areas of the human body. Instead, it paved the way towards his main

"Benjamin Franklin Drawing Electricity from the Sky", by Benjamin West, 1816.
It commemorates a 1752 experiment in Philadelphia, in which Franklin
demonstrated that lightning is a form of electricity. (Image: Philadelphia Museum of Art.)

electrical invention, the lightning rod. Franklin later said he'd lost confidence in using electricity as a therapy for patients.

However, Franklin's international stature further intensified a craze in Europe for electrical phenomena as an entertainment in polite society. In darkened salons performers choreographed displays of flashing lights, sparks and shocks. Men and women paid to watch their hair stand on end, or their hands attract pieces of paper.[73]

Women were deemed essential participants in the spectacle. One favourite trick in public demonstrations became known as the "electrifying Venus", or "electric kiss". A lady volunteer would stand on an insulated stool, while the demonstrator used an electrical machine to charge her body. Gentlemen in the audience were then invited to kiss her. As they approached her lips, a strong spark would repel any such attempt, much to the amusement and titillation of all.

Audiences soon became receptive to the idea of this newly discovered electrical "fire" also having the power to heal. Shocks and sparks for a therapeutic purpose were added to the spectacle, which became more about curing people, rather than just providing a few cheap thrills.

It was during a supper party in Bristol, at the home of her medical friend John Till Adams, that Sarah Champion Fox agreed to receive an electric shock as therapy. She hated the experience. However, some patients really believed it could work. Paola Bertucci explained its popular appeal, in a paper on medical electricity in eighteenth century London:

"Medical electricity was advocated by its supporters as a therapy that anyone could pursue. It was cheap, since its only cost was that of the electrical machine (that could be shared among neighbours) and it did not require medical knowledge. Directions on how to administer electric shocks or other forms of electrical therapies could be obtained from published pamphlets."[74]

In a Diary entry for October 1782, Sarah Champion Fox reported visiting the house of a female friend. There she came across Shurmer Bath *"trying the effect of electricity on CP, who had an increasing stiffness in her joints"*.[75]

"CP" was Sarah's long-standing friend Catherine Philips (1726-1794), a Quaker minister and travelling preacher. She was an intrepid woman, who for about 45 years trekked around the British Isles, Holland and America, covering

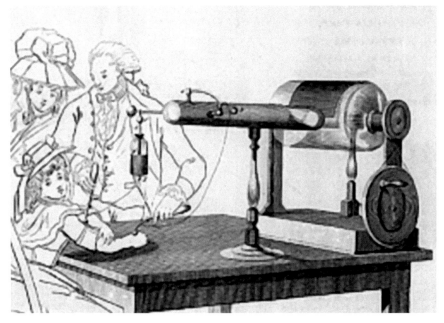

The frontispiece of George Adams's 'An Essay on Electricity', published in 1785.

some 9,000 miles in total. In America she and a female companion had visited plantations with slave labour in North Carolina. The experience turned her into a radical supporter of abolition.[76]

Catherine's appointment with Shurmer Bath tells us not only that he, too, had acquired his own machine for electrical treatment, but also that it was a portable one, small and light enough for carrying to other people's homes. In fact, "Dr" Bath had already been experimenting on his patients with electricity for at least 20 years. *The Diary of William Dyer* has this casual one-line entry for 27 May 1762:

"This afternoon called on Shurmer Bath and saw some electrical experiments. Drank tea at home."[77]

William Dyer was another amateur doctor treating some of his patients with electricity.

He was eight years older than Shurmer, who in 1762 was still only 23. To modern minds it's quite horrifying that self-taught young men were dabbling in electric shocks, trying them out for any therapeutic effect on people they knew in the community. Yet the pair had very good company in their well intentioned but risky experiments.

An electrical machine that was portable, simpler to operate and came in a box had recently been designed and built in London by a young technician called John Read. The apprentice of a cabinet maker, he needed a remedy himself for violent pains at the back of his neck.

It was 1758, coinciding exactly with the period Shurmer Bath spent in London, apprenticed to a patten maker. Both lads had carpentry skills and a shared interest in medicine. It's possible that Shurmer bought his own portable machine from John Read and carried it back to Bristol.[78]

In a 1760 Diary entry Shurmer's fellow amateur doctor William Dyer reported that several Bristol surgeons had bought electrical machines. One was installed at the Bristol Infirmary and another at St Peter's Hospital, medical wing of the workhouse for "paupers".[79]

William's own use of the technique began that year, 1760. From then onwards, for him, treating his patients with electricity for their aches and pains became almost routine.

For example, a Diary entry on 9 October 1762 starts very casually: *"Rose near 7. Electrised Miss Hawkswell & also Capt Purchase."*[80]

For 15 November Dyer writes: *"At 5 home where was Mr Brown who staid 'till p[ast] 6 & was electrised for strain of his instep..."*[81]

On 20 November he reports: *"...visited Mother Davis & electrised her toe with my small machine..."*[82]

27 December: *"This morning electrised Mr Barnett".*[83]

It may be significant that in general William Dyer used pills and *"decoctions"* for the most serious cases, when it was a matter of life and death. He also sometimes consulted, or acted in tandem with, a qualified doctor if he felt greater expertise was needed.

William mainly reserved the electrical machine for pain relief from minor injuries, or conditions like gout and rheumatism. He claimed to be the first practitioner in Bristol to buy one himself and use it for medical treatment. If so, Shurmer Bath must have followed close behind.

ELECTRIFYING PREACHERS

William Dyer enjoyed going to church and he liked to ring the changes. His restless and inquiring mind often took him beyond the confines of his own Anglican environment. He might, perhaps, attend a Quaker meeting or a Methodist sermon, especially when the preacher was John Wesley, whom he knew.

William's closest personal friend was the Rev. Richard Symes (1722-1799), Rector of St Werburgh's. The 1762 Dyer Diary is packed with references to the clergyman. Richard Symes, an Oxford graduate, belonged to the evangelical wing of the Church of England, and practised electrical healing. He even wrote a book about it, *Fire Analysed*, published in Bristol in 1771. William often joined his friend's congregation at services.[84]

St Werburgh's Church stood in Corn Street, in the heart of the old city. This was long before the building was moved, stone by stone, to its present location in a suburb of the same name. Rev. Symes ran his tiny parish for 45 years from 1754, attracting a congregation of like-minded Bristolians from all over the city.

Many of them were also *"electrised"* by him in the literal sense. By July 1760 Richard Symes had an electrical machine made for him, based on the design already used by William Dyer. The second half of Symes's book on the subject comprises an account of case studies – individual patients he'd allegedly cured with his machine.

Among evangelicals and religious dissenters in Bristol, this confidence in electricity as a healer and curer was more a matter of faith than objective analysis. In cases where there was little or no effect, practitioners simply moved on to the next patient. The clergy now embracing this new miracle believed with utter conviction that the sparks and shocks were a gift from God, sent for the benefit of mankind.[85]

They saw the sparks created by an electrical charge as "fire" from the heavens, giving people on earth a new opportunity to relieve physical suffering. It was, therefore, a duty to harness that divine fire and use it to heal the sick at every opportunity.

St Werburgh's Church, now an indoor climbing centre. In 1877 the building was demolished on its former site in Corn Street, central Bristol, because it made the road too narrow for carriages. The stones were transported to a new location in Mina Road, about two miles away, where the church was reconstructed.

This printed engraving of Corn Street in 1829 shows the original position of St Werburgh's Church, in the background on the right.
(Image: courtesy of Bristol Archives, 40145/Dr/17.)

Some practitioners drew their inspiration from the writings of a lay clerk at Worcester Cathedral. Richard Lovett (1692-1780) published a series of works on electricity. William Dyer, Shurmer Bath and many other devotees subscribed to Lovett's *Philosophical Essays* on the subject, published in 1766. Dyer twice went to visit Lovett in Worcester.

By far the most high-profile advocate of electrical therapy among clergymen was John Wesley (1703-1791). He even experimented with it on himself. The leader of the Methodist movement was a travelling preacher, born in Lincolnshire. However, Bristol became his adopted home city for many years.

Wesley's "New Room" chapel in Broadmead, built in 1739, was the first of many he established in London and elsewhere. Within a decade it had to be doubled in size to meet local demand. The Bristol chapel was designed for multi-purpose community use, with a suite of rooms upstairs to accommodate

The New Room in Broadmead, built in 1739 and expanded in 1748 to meet demand.
(Photo: The New Room Bristol website)

Wesley and visiting preachers. It served as Wesley's home base for almost 30 years in the mid 1700s.[86]

The chapel also had enough space for a schoolroom and a free dispensary, or clinic, for the poorest patients. This arrangement was separate from the larger Bristol Dispensary on Stokes Croft, which also offered free healthcare to the poor when it opened in 1775. (There will be more on the Bristol Dispensary in Chapter 8.)

John Wesley was respected, and even loved, by people from all Christian denominations and social classes. They flocked to hear him preach sermons calling for reform of the established Church, stricter moral values and abolition of the slave trade. Wesley adopted many causes during a long and varied life. His fervent support for treating patients with electricity is often overlooked and deserves to be far better known.

Wesley became a convert as early as 1753, after watching a public demonstration with some friends. History doesn't tell us whether it involved an "electric kiss"! He was immediately intrigued, but perplexed curiosity soon turned to a passionate conviction that here was a cheap and easy way to treat

'John Wesley Preaching before the Mayor and Corporation of Bristol, 1788', painted by William Holt Yates Titcomb (1858-1930.) (Image: courtesy of Bristol Culture, Bristol Museum & Art Gallery, K519)

many illnesses.[87] In November 1756 Wesley reported in his *Journal* that he had obtained a portable electrical apparatus for use in London.

He wrote: *"I ordered several persons to be electrified, who were ill of various disorders, some of whom found an immediate, some a gradual cure. From this time I appointed, first some hours in every week, and afterward an hour in every day, wherein any that desired it might try the virtue of this surprising medicine...and to this day, while hundreds, perhaps thousands, have received unspeakable good, I have not known one man, woman, or child, who has received hurt thereby."*[88]

Wesley also experimented with the machine on himself, using electric shock treatment for his own lameness and neuralgia. His motivation was partly to combat doctors, whom he saw as greedy profiteers overcharging for medicine. He put electrical machines in all his free dispensaries, of which there were three in London, as well as the one in Bristol. The electrotherapy done there and in other places resulted in a book by Wesley on the subject. It was published in 1760 as *The Desideratum: Or, Electricity made Plain and Useful by a Lover of Mankind and of Common Sense.*

Like William Dyer and Richard Symes, Wesley was a pragmatist. He applied what seemed to work and didn't bother much about explaining how. He believed electricity was created by God for the good of mankind and it was His will that people should use it.

Wesley tried electricity on himself again in old age. His *Journal* records two occasions, once when he was 70 and the other when he'd reached 80. On a preaching tour of the West Country in September 1773, Wesley had a severe pain in his shoulder and side and could barely lift his hand to his face. He asked assistants to electrify him - and later felt well enough to preach his sermon.[89]

A decade later Wesley caught a bad cold, resulting in a deep cough that wouldn't go away. He carried on preaching from one town to another, but felt very weak and developed a fever. He suffered painful cramp in his legs and a tight chest. Wesley persuaded a friend to electrify him several times a day in these areas of the body, and recovered enough to resume preaching.

In his book, *The Desideratum*, Wesley gave 49 examples of other cases where electrification allegedly resulted in a cure. These are a few of them:[90]

"Anne Heathcot...was seized, in May last, with what is commonly called an Ague in the Head, having a violent Pain in her Head, Face and Teeth. After trying abundance of Remedies, to no purpose, she was, in August, electrified thro' the Head. Immediately the Pain fix'd in her Teeth. She was electrified four Times more, and has felt nothing of it since."

"William Jones, a Plaisterer, ...fell from a Scaffold on Thursday, Feb.15 last. He was grievously bruised, both outwardly and inwardly, and lay in violent pain, utterly helpless, till Saturday in the Afternoon, when he was brought (carried) by two men to be electrified. After a few Minutes he walk'd home alone, and on Monday went to work."

"Elizabeth Collis, a Child of twelve Years old...was so far gone in a genuine Consumption, that she was judg'd to be quite past Recovery. This Summer she was electrified four Times, and has been quite well ever since."

"A Boy about seven Years old (says Mr Floyer, a surgeon in Dorchester) was taken blind suddenly in both his Eyes, without any previous Pain or Fever. Three or four Days after, he was brought to me...I told his parents, it was my Opinion he would never see again. However I determined to try the Electric Shock: And the next Morning fastened a Wire coming from the Phial to his Leg, and another round his Head, I brought the Latter near the Conductor, and gave him four

Shocks successively. That Day he was put to Bed...till the next Morning, when he agreeably alarmed his Father by crying out, he could see the Window...This gave me Encouragement to repeat what we had done the Day before...the Third Day he could distinguish Objects; the Fourth, Colours. The Fifth Day, after repeating the Experiment, his Sight was perfectly restor'd, and the Eyes, in every Respect, as well as if no Disorder had happened to them."

Wesley also listed a total of 37 ailments in which, he claimed, electrification had been found to be *"of unquestionable use"*:[91]

Agues	*Hysterics*
St Anthony's Fire	*Inflammations*
Blindness	*King's Evil*
Blood extravasated	*Knots in the Flesh*
Bronchocele	*Lameness, Leprosy*
Chlorosis	*Mortification*
Coldness in the feet	*Palpitation of the Heart*
Consumption	*Pain in the back, in the Stomach*
Contractions of the limbs	*Palsy, Pleurisy*
Cramp	*Rheumatism, Ring worms*
Deafness, Dropsy	*Sciatica, Shingles, Sprain*
Epilepsy	*Surfeit*
Feet violently disorder'd	*Swellings of all Kinds*
Felons	*Throat sore*
Fistula Lacrymalis	*Toe hurt*
Fits, Ganglions, Gout, Gravel	*Tooth-Ache*
Head ache	*Wen*

However, Wesley wasn't entirely gung-ho about electrical therapy. At the end of *The Desideratum* he does warn his readers to be careful how it's done:

"In order to prevent any ill Effect, these two cautions should always be remembered. First, let not the Shock be too violent, rather let several small Shocks be given. Secondly, do not give a Shock to the whole Body, when only a small Part is affected. If it be given to the Part affected only, little Harm can follow even from a violent Shock." [92]

PREACHING TO THE CONVERTED

What are we to make of these extraordinary claims by Wesley about using electricity to cure so many varied diseases? From our twenty-first century standpoint most of us would dismiss them as belonging to the realm of fantasy and fake news. Surely we can't give any credence to something we know is ludicrous and impossible?

This conclusion brings more questions. Did John Wesley really believe in these miracle cures himself? Was he a liar, who deliberately made it all up to popularise his religious agenda? Or was he more like a spin doctor of his time, manipulating the facts to demonstrate the power of God among ignorant and gullible people?

For example, in his book *The Desideratum* Wesley refers only to the success stories among those treated, barely mentioning any failures. By contrast, the lay amateur practitioner William Dyer frankly admits it in his Diary when his treatment goes wrong or proves ineffective. If electrotherapy really did work, why aren't doctors still using it now, to cure anything from blindness to a sore throat?

Of course, in the twenty-first century we have the benefit of hindsight. It's much easier for us to dismiss the case made by Wesley and other evangelists than to explain their faith in electric shocks as a multi-purpose remedy. We should bear in mind that although this treatment never became mainstream, neither was it generally thought of as outlandish or weird.

In Bristol a number of respected and progressive doctors, like the Quaker John Till Adams, bought an electrical machine to try on their patients. St Peter's Hospital, for paupers, had one available in the 1760s. In London the machines were used quite widely in people's homes and in some hospitals, like St Thomas's, as well as in the Wesley free clinics.

There were other important factors, too. In the eighteenth century many ordinary men and women had their own ideas on remedies for self-healing, especially plants and herbal concoctions. It was normal for the public to try a bit of DIY healthcare on themselves and their family or friends.[93]

In her book *Patients, Power and the Poor in Eighteenth Century Bristol*, Mary Fissell summed up this tradition of medical self-help in the community:

"Many understood how to maintain health and treat illness; medical knowledge was a part of everyday discourse. There were wig-makers, blood-letters, inoculators, itinerant venereal disease doctors, druggists and 'cunning women', purveying health care which competed with domestic medicine provided by patients themselves."

In Bristol attitudes were gradually changing to "doctor knows best", via the introduction of structured hospital training for students at the Infirmary. However, John Wesley greatly resented the physicians, surgeons and apothecaries who so often overprescribed and overcharged for medicine. He liked electricity partly because it was free and avoided the expense of a doctor.[94]

Traditional beliefs in the supernatural, including even witchcraft, to ward off ailments or cause sickness still persisted to some extent. Even the multi-talented practitioner John Till Adams was deeply interested in astrology to guide the dispensing of medicines.[95] Astrological charts and tables, showing the position of the moon and stars, were also used by some doctors to determine the most appropriate time for bleeding a patient. It wasn't a huge leap from astrology to faith in electricity, or *"divine fire"*, as a healing agent.

One example of the old superstitions still carrying some influence was Thomas Perks, from Mangotsfield near Bristol. He was a blacksmith in the early 1700s, who studied astrology and, supposedly, conversed with spirits. Perks invited a local clergyman to come and see them. He drew a chalk circle at a crossroads, chanted words from the Bible and allegedly produced several tiny women, 18 inches high. Perks later recounted losing control of the spirits and being troubled by *"dismal Shapes, like Serpents, Lions, Bears etc, and hissing at him, or attempting to throw spears, or Balls of Fire at him".*[96]

The diarist Sarah Champion Fox, in a 1761 letter to her brother Richard, related another strange tale about magic, which she was told by a man at work in a field.

"As he was just going to work with his fellow labourers, it happened that he found a white wand and when they went home they burnt this white wand, and so a little while after the old woman who own'd it came to discover the matter, that this man dreadful to relate fell sick, so that they could find no relief till a Neighbour more knowing than the rest found out the Cause and nature of his Distemper and told him he was bewitch'd."

Sarah commented that she found it amazing how superstitious country people still were. It was an age of inquiring minds and willingness to experiment with both the old and the new. In this febrile environment the idea of harnessing divine fire from the heavens for therapeutic purposes may not have seemed all that far-fetched.

One can understand devout members of a congregation truly believing in electricity as a powerful healing agent sent by God, if a charismatic minister preached that message. There may even have been a "placebo effect", which is known to happen sometimes in modern medicine. A patient is given a dummy pill in a clinical trial, but doesn't know this and feels the same benefits as someone given the real drug. However, as a theory to explain the dramatic scale of recoveries claimed by John Wesley, it seems very implausible.

CHAPTER 7

THE GEORGIAN SCOURGE

All of us who've endured the Covid-19 pandemic know the feeling that it's going on forever and that lockdown restrictions might become the new normal. How would we cope if its deadly impact lasted not just a few years but a whole century, or even longer? The late 1600s and early 1700s saw a sharp rise in smallpox cases across Europe. It became a major cause of death in Britain until the nineteenth century. The disease was highly infectious, very painful and spread fast among all social classes.

Smallpox accounted for five to 20 per cent of all burials in British cities and left many of the survivors permanently scarred or blind. It became endemic in London. In the worst outbreaks one in five people who caught the disease died, with children especially vulnerable. Smallpox created a tremendous fear because it was lethal and there seemed no escape from it.[97]

Everything started to change right at the end of the eighteenth century. It happened thanks to the ingenuity and perseverance of a doctor in the quiet country town of Berkeley in Gloucestershire, a few miles north of Bristol. Dr Edward Jenner (1749-1823) proved that what he called a vaccine gave protection against smallpox.

Jenner knew of an old saying in folklore that if you caught cowpox, a mild form of the disease, from your cows, then you couldn't get smallpox. In May 1796 a Berkeley

Portrait of Edward Jenner
(Image: St George's, University of London)

Jenner House and Museum, Berkeley

dairymaid, Sarah Nelmes, consulted him about a rash on her hand. Jenner diagnosed cowpox and decided to test its protective capability on someone who hadn't yet fallen victim to the far more dangerous smallpox.[98]

He chose James Phipps, the eight-year-old son of his gardener. James was deliberately infected with cowpox by rubbing matter from the pocks on Sarah's hand into incisions made on his arm. The boy became mildly ill from cowpox, but soon recovered. Jenner then inoculated him with matter from smallpox pustules and, as anticipated, James stayed healthy.

The doctor had proved that cowpox infection was a safe way to achieve immunity from smallpox. He coined the word "vaccine" for it, from the Latin *vacca* for cow.

I've always felt a strong personal affinity with Jenner. My own birthplace, Berkeley Hospital (now permanently closed), stands right opposite the house where he was born in 1749. I was brought up on a farm near the town in the 1950s and 60s. Some of the farm's land is rented from the Berkeley Castle Estate. My late mother used to be a guide at the castle.

Jenner's breakthrough against smallpox gave him a lasting place as one of the great innovators in medical science history. His vaccine led eventually to the World Health Organisation officially declaring the disease to have been eradicated in 1980. It's been estimated that the work he started has saved

Portrait of Benjamin Jesty by Michael W. Sharp, 1805. (Image: Wellcome Library. Reproduced under Creative Commons Attribution only licence CC BY 4.0)

more lives than that of any other person.[99]

Jenner's stature as the father of vaccination has been enhanced even more by the coronavirus pandemic. It was Jenner who did the original groundwork that has enabled teams of scientists worldwide to develop effective vaccines so quickly against this new modern scourge.

It would be wrong, though, to give Jenner all the credit. In fact, a North Dorset farmer beat him to it as the first vaccinator - by 22 years. Benjamin Jesty (1737-1816), from the village of Yetminster, had also known the story about milkmaids and their apparent immunity from smallpox. In 1774 he experimented by taking material from the udders of his cows and scratching it into the arms of his wife and two boys. The trio subsequently remained free of smallpox for life.[100]

Benjamin Jesty won official recognition in 1805 from the science establishment, but the farmer had never pursued his initial successful

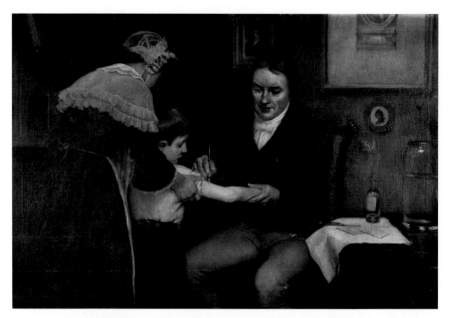

Dr Edward Jenner performing his first experimental vaccination in 1796, as portrayed a century later by the artist Ernest Board. (Image: Wellcombe Library. Reproduced under Creative Commons Attribution only licence CC BY 4.0)

experiment. In addition to this precedent, Jenner also received a little help from his friends down the road in Bristol.

JENNER AND THE LUDLOWS OF BRISTOL

Edward Jenner was born in Berkeley, the eighth of nine children. His father was the Vicar of Berkeley, the Rev. Stephen Jenner. The boy went to school in another small Gloucestershire town, Wotton-under-Edge. At the age of 14 Jenner was apprenticed for seven years to a surgeon, Daniel Ludlow (born in 1720). He was from a Quaker family in nearby Chipping Sodbury, and ran a successful medical practice there. With him Jenner gained most of the experience needed to acquire similar skills. In 1770 he went on to study at the prestigious St George's Hospital in London, before resettling in Berkeley as a local practitioner.[101]

Much earlier, from 1735, Daniel Ludlow had been an apprentice to his own uncle, Abraham Ludlow senior (1708-1753), who was a surgeon in Bristol. Ludlow senior's son, also called Abraham, was to become a key figure on the city's medical and social scene. As Daniel's cousin, Abraham Ludlow junior would have known Jenner, who was 12 years younger than him, via these apprenticeship and family links. It's likely that all three men exchanged ideas on each other's work.[102]

Dr Abraham Ludlow junior (1737-1807) was also a pioneer in the fight to curb smallpox, 30 years before Jenner's final breakthrough. He and two colleagues set up an *"inoculating house"* at Barton Hill, which in those days was a rural retreat just outside Bristol. The inoculation centre's existence was rediscovered through the modern publication of Sarah Champion Fox's Diary. In her chronicles of daily life, for 20 March 1768, Sarah wrote:

"Went with my niece and nephew...to the inoculating house at Barton Hill, opened by one of Sutton's partners, Abraham Ludlow & John Ford."[103]

In the 1720s, when no-one had yet thought of using cowpox for protection against smallpox, a few British surgeons and senior doctors began experimenting with inoculation, mainly on children. Rudimentary forms of a similar technique had been practised for centuries in parts of Asia and Africa. Otherwise known as variolation, it meant deliberately infecting patients with smallpox, in the hope of producing a mild form of the disease in the short term and immunity in future.[104]

They made incisions with a needle and applied residue from smallpox pustules into the wound. Variolation was just as likely to induce severe smallpox as would a natural infection, and could prove fatal. Edward Jenner later credited his childhood experience of being variolated in Wotton-under-Edge for making him aware of its hazards. When he became a local doctor, Jenner administered variolations/inoculations on his own patients.[105]

Fees for a jab could be very high, especially as they covered food, board and lodging in an isolation house, plus the attendance of a practitioner and nurse for a month. Few families could afford the cost of an inoculation, apart from the gentry.

The Sutton referred to in Sarah's Diary was Robert Sutton, a country practitioner from Suffolk. In the mid eighteenth century he created a new and improved technique for inoculation. Robert and his son, Daniel Sutton, popularised the so-called "Suttonian method", but at first kept secret exactly what it involved.[106]

In fact, they were using a cleaner and sharper lancet to make smaller incisions. The patients, mainly children, were no longer starved and bled beforehand, but instead given a normal diet in cool conditions. The procedure was far less painful and much safer than before. However, the Suttons withheld information about it from other medics, except those willing to sign up as a partner.

By 1768, when Sarah Champion Fox made her Diary entry, the Suttons had about 50 partners around Britain and even as far away as Jamaica and Virginia. One of them was a surgeon from Ipswich called John Rodbard. Abraham Ludlow and John Ford, both surgeons at the Bristol Infirmary, teamed up with Rodbard to open their *"inoculating house"* at Barton Hill. Sarah's Diary goes on to describe it:

"... a very commodious house fitted for the reception of any patients, & under good regulations. After the operation we brought them home till they sickened, and then sent them back with a servant who was to be subject to the rules of the house." [107]

Two weeks later Sarah added a rather complacent note about the outcome: *"April 4th. The children being pretty well, whom we had seen most afternoons at the inoculating house, I went to Stoke [Bishop] for the summer."*

Presumably, the children were Sarah's niece and nephew, whom she'd taken for this new jab given by her trusted family doctor.

The 1760s saw a nationwide explosion in demand for smallpox inoculations, thanks to the Sutton family's inventiveness, hard work and keen business sense. Daniel Sutton claimed to have inoculated 22,000 people himself between 1763 and 1766, with only three deaths. The new method still failed to provide immunity from smallpox, but mitigated its effects and reduced the numbers dying from it. [108]

In Bristol, as elsewhere, there was initial opposition from practitioners offering smallpox inoculations themselves, for a hefty price. For example, the apothecary William Broderip charged three to five guineas per jab . That would be between £500 and £800 in today's money. Imagine the cost if you had 10 children, which was not unusual then. [109]

However, Daniel Sutton attracted widespread popular support nationally. His rivals could no longer deny the improvements from his method, which became standard across the country. With mass inoculation now in prospect, the fees dropped to half a guinea, then halved to five shillings, and even reduced to zero for a while in some cases.[110]

FIRST VACCINE PASSPORT

Attitudes in Bristol no doubt changed when the high-profile Abraham Ludlow came on board, as part of an experienced team doing inoculations the Sutton way at Barton Hill.

It was a major step forward, but soon largely forgotten - because along came Jenner with his light bulb moment that eclipsed everything, and everyone, before it.

Even so, Jenner had to fight for recognition of his cowpox vaccine from the medical and scientific establishment in London. He replicated his successful experiment with James Phipps in 20 or so other local cases in Berkeley, including his own infant son Robert. Jenner wrote a paper on his findings, which the Royal Society rejected. They wouldn't take seriously a rustic doctor's

James Gillray's 1802 caricature of Edward Jenner vaccinating patients, who feared it would make them sprout cow-like appendages.

Portrait of Thomas Jefferson by Rembrandt Peale, 1800

theory, based on a minor illness caught by milkmaids from cows. As a result, Jenner had to publish the findings himself in 1798. A savagely satirical caricature by Gillray in 1802 also influenced public opinion against him.

Despite official disapproval in London, news of Jenner's successful experiment spread fast in Europe and America. The Berkeley doctor sent his vaccine to medical acquaintances who asked for it. In 1800 one sample reached a professor of medicine at Harvard University, Benjamin Waterhouse, who persuaded Thomas Jefferson, the US Vice President and future President, to test it out.

Thomas Jefferson (1743-1826) was a keen amateur scientist and owned Monticello, a vast plantation estate in Virginia with 400 slaves. He was supplied with the cowpox vaccine by Waterhouse and trialled it first on three of his slaves at Monticello. Clearly, to Jefferson black lives were expendable in the cause of medical research.

However, that initial experiment on his slaves worked. About 200 people from Jefferson's extended family, including sons-in-law and some neighbours, were then vaccinated. When exposed to smallpox in the next few months, none of them caught it.[111]

Jefferson's own clinical trial convinced him the vaccine was safe and effective. After becoming President in 1801, he openly supported American doctors in establishing the new method and in working towards mass vaccination across the United States.

The Thomas Jefferson approach couldn't have been more different from that of President Donald Trump towards the Covid-19 pandemic, two centuries later in 2020. Trump was in denial that the virus posed a serious threat to the US public and dragged his feet over action to combat its spread.

A WARD IN THE HAMPSTEAD SMALLPOX HOSPITAL.

Nurses and patients at Hampstead Smallpox Hospital, from the illustrated London News, 1871.
(Image: Wellcome Library. Reproduced under Creative Commons Attribution only licence CC BY 4.0)

Vaccination was slower to catch on in Britain. Only after a long campaign by Jenner and his supporters did it eventually win official acceptance. In 1840 the government banned variolation (the other word for inoculation) as a protective method against smallpox. In 1853, three decades after Edward Jenner's death, the cowpox vaccine was made free and mandatory by law for all babies.

Under the Vaccination Act it became compulsory for all children born after 1 August 1853 to be vaccinated against smallpox during their first three months of life. Parents who failed, or refused, to get it done would be subject to a fine of one pound. By the 1860s two thirds of babies were receiving the jab. The smallpox death toll was falling at last as a result.[112]

Mass vaccination had arrived. It was thanks to the efforts of a country doctor near Bristol - and a network of other talented practitioners, who did some important spadework before Jenner's innovation changed the world.

The new legislation also required a certificate to be provided after every vaccination, giving the parents or guardian of that child a document to prove that it had been done. It was the responsibility of the doctor who gave the jab to issue the certificate, a copy of which also went to the local registrar's office.

A Bristol historian, John Penny, still has the certificate for his great-grandfather's smallpox vaccination as an infant in 1858. It was an early form of the vaccine passport which, more than 150 years later, became an issue in the Covid pandemic. One difference between then and now, however, was that in Victorian times the smallpox vaccination was compulsory. Therefore, a certificate - or the lack of one - could be used by the authorities in court to prove non-compliance, or by parents to avoid a fine. That it was admissible as evidence is explained on the back of the document itself (See the second of the two images on page 89).

COMPULSORY VACCINATION ACT.
(16 & 17 Victoria, Cap. 100.)

SCHEDULE A.

Medical Certificate of Successful Vaccination.

[To be delivered (pursuant to Section IV.) to the Father or Mother of every Child successfully Vaccinated, or to the Person having the Care, Nurture, or Custody of such Child.]

I, the undersigned, hereby certify, That

(ª) *John Penny* (aged (ᵇ) *3 Months*),

the Child of (ᶜ) *Thomas Penny* of (ᵈ) [and residing at

No. *8* in *Hacott Parade* Street in]

the Parish of *St. Peters*

in the County of *Bristol* has been successfully vaccinated by me.

Dated this (ᵉ) *14ᵗʰ* day of *May* 185*8* .

(Signature of the Person certifying) *Alfred Smith*

(Add Professional Titles) *MRCS & LAC*

[☞ See Note on the other side.]

☞ This Certificate should be carefully preserved by the Parents of the within-named Child ; it being, without further proof, admissible as evidence of the successful Vaccination of the Child in any Information or Complaint which shall be brought against the Father or Mother of the Child ; or against the Person who shall have had the Care, Nurture, or Custody of such Child, for non-compliance with the provisions of the within-mentioned Act. (Section IV.)

This vaccination certificate issued in Bristol for John Penny, aged three months, in 1858 has been reproduced courtesy of his great- grandson of the same name. It was the vaccine "passport" of its time.

CHAPTER 8

PAUPER HOSPITAL

It's already clear from this snapshot of eighteenth century medicine in and around Bristol that there was an aching void, ready for philanthropists and amateur practitioners like Shurmer Bath to fill. People living in deprivation - in other words, most people - simply couldn't afford to call out a trained doctor or pay for medicine. In a cut-throat health market, driven by private enterprise and moderated only by charity, there was an enormous gap between the haves and have-nots.

Evidence about "Dr" Bath's policy is scarce, but it seems he mainly wanted to help the "deserving" poor - the ones who worked hard, behaved themselves and went to church, chapel or meeting house. Shurmer must have made quite an impact in Bristol to merit the glowing obituary he received in a national magazine after his death in 1800. (See Chapter 2.) He was also exceptional, even among Quakers, in being both a medical practitioner and a key charity organiser.

Nevertheless, despite Shurmer Bath's free pills and electric shocks, and all the efforts of other do-gooders, the masses in Bristol still had very limited access to healthcare. St Peter's Hospital provided it free to the utterly destitute from 1698. It stood in a lane behind St Peter's Church in the old city. This magnificent medieval building was originally a merchant's grand residence, dating back to the 1400s. Much later on both house and church would be left in ruins by the Bristol Blitz in the Second World War.[113]

In the seventeenth century part of the mansion became a sugar refinery. Then it served briefly as the Mint. When the building was converted into St Peter's Hospital in 1698, it was really an early workhouse, which took in "paupers", including their children and the aged. A medical wing was incorporated for inmates who fell sick.

St Peter's was called a hospital in the sense of a place of refuge, rather than

Watercolour drawing of St Peter's Hospital by Mary Katherine Moore, 1894.
(Image: courtesy of Bristol Culture, Bristol Museum & Art Gallery, K373)

a medical facility, although it did have one. Funding came from the Bristol Poor Act in 1696, the first legislation of its kind in England. It created a union of parishes to pay for housing and feeding the poorest families, in return for the inmates' hard labour.[114]

Unlike London and the old-established Scottish universities, Bristol had no medical school of its own until 1833. For this reason surgeons often worked at St Peter's Hospital at the start of their career, to provide the training and experience for a job application to the Infirmary.

DOCTOR IN THE HOUSE

For those just above the bottom of the heap in Bristol, there was no such guaranteed free medical care until the 1730s, with the opening of a purpose-built Infirmary.

Enter Dr Abraham Ludlow. His work doing smallpox inoculations at Barton Hill has already been outlined in Chapter 7. He was the son of a surgeon, also named Abraham. However, it's worth exploring this enigmatic character in more detail. The first impression is of a pompous, arrogant and vain self-publicist, obsessed with being respected as a high-ranking physician.[115]

Ludlow junior was educated at Taunton Grammar School, before being apprenticed to his father. When Ludlow senior died in 1753, the apprenticeship was transferred to another Bristol surgeon, John Page. Later, in 1767, Abraham was elected to the post of surgeon at the Bristol Infirmary. In 1771 he obtained a medical degree from St Andrews University, which qualified him as a physician. This took him above surgeons in the Infirmary pecking order. It also entitled Ludlow to put "Dr" in front of his name and the letters "M.D." after it.

A rigid hierarchy at the Infirmary led to outbursts of jealousy among senior colleagues, their quarrels sometimes spilling into violence. There were fisticuffs and even the occasional duel. Relations between Abraham Ludlow and individual rivals grew especially tense. There was a strong suspicion, voiced by one or two of the medics, that he may simply have written a letter to St Andrews asking for his degree, rather than doing anything to earn it. In other words, promotion by mail order!

Richard Smith junior, the surgeon who wrote down for posterity his reminiscences of past and present colleagues at the Infirmary, made this observation about Dr Ludlow:

"He had cultivated a stately and pompous walk, with a stiff, stand-off manner, and his enormous wig...was in itself most imposing." [116]

In the eighteenth century most hospital physicians and surgeons still wore a sword or rapier at work. Richard Smith added more detail in this description of Dr Ludlow on his ward rounds:

"He was distinguished from the common mass by an imposing exterior. He moved with a measured step and affected a meditative countenance, with a pomposity of diction and manners which could not but keep the vulgar at a respectable distance." [117]

According to the Infirmary chronicler, Dr Ludlow bore a strong physical resemblance to his famous contemporary Dr Samuel Johnson. There's a rough charcoal-drawn illustration of Ludlow in A *History of the Bristol Royal Infirmary*. It was probably sketched by Richard Smith or a colleague. So, in

Johnson   Ludlow

tribute to the deliberately reversed "lookalikes" that feature in the satirical magazine *Private Eye*, let's compare the sketch with a portrait of Dr Johnson by Sir Joshua Reynolds.

I wonder if they were by any chance related! The most striking impression from Dr Ludlow's air of inflated self-importance - of course, he's really the one on the left - is that it was so untypical of Quakers and their behaviour. They advocated modesty, self-effacement and peaceful coexistence.

Alongside his career at the Infirmary, Ludlow ran a lucrative private practice from home at 12 Cumberland Street, St Pauls, and from premises in nearby Brunswick Square. When he rose to the level of physician, his work as a family doctor expanded so much that in 1774 he gave up the Infirmary job, after seven years in post.

In a resignation letter sent from Brunswick Square, he said it was on the grounds that *"his engagements in Physick"* had made him decide to *"decline the practical part of surgery"*.[118] It made little difference financially, since the Infirmary roles were honorary and intended as a gateway to, or addition to, private practice.

Dr Ludlow was a man of immense energy with a massive workload, constantly in demand. His medical practice alone earned him £2,500 a year (equivalent to £400,000 now). This was mainly in small fees from a large

Dr Abraham Ludlow lived at 12 Cumberland Street, St Pauls, for many years from the 1770s. The house stood to the right of those shown, but is no longer there.

number of patients. The flamboyant Quaker devised an unusual, but easily recognisable, calling card to advertise himself and show off the demand for his services. He would put down straw in front of all houses where he was treating a seriously ill person. The number of streets with straw on them demonstrated the extent of his business.[119]

Dr Ludlow's private practice reached far beyond the cluster of his mainly affluent fellow Quakers. However, he was constantly available on call to the diarist Sarah Champion Fox, plus her family and social circle. Ludlow was a personal friend to some of them, including Sarah herself, as well as being their family doctor. They clearly liked and trusted him. This doctor became the one to call in a life-or-death emergency, which was all too common.

Chapter 5 has already referred to Sarah's gratitude for Dr Ludlow's "skill and attention" in enabling the recovery of her friend Sally Young from a "putrid fever" [typhoid]. Diary entries for April 1781 again portray Dr Ludlow in a favourable light. He was caring for the wealthy banker Mark Harford on his deathbed, probably at 2 King Square. Harford, who was only 43, had been ill for a couple of months.

Sarah Champion Fox describes the scene in extraordinarily intimate and moving detail. Her Diary shows that individual personal relationships among the rich Quaker banking, merchant and industrial families of Bristol – on this occasion the Champions, Harfords and Lloyds – could be very close:

"April 4th. Heard that Mark Harford was worse, & that Dr Ludlow was sent for."

"29th....Just as I was retired to my chamber for the night, I received a note from Dr Ludlow desiring I would come immediately to M.Harford's, for it was not probable he would live through the night. On my approaching his bedside, I found him in a dying state. He appeared insensible and groaned incessantly. I accompanied his wife into another room & sat with her the whole night. Once he seemed a little revived but soon relapsed – lived only till about 8 o'clock the next morning. I had sent the coach for M. Lloyd, but she did not arrive till our valued friend had breathed his last, whom I had too long known & esteemed not to feel on the occasion. The constant intercourse we had from childhood had, at a maturer age, ripened into friendship."[120]

DOCTOR IN THE DISPENSARY

Dr Ludlow had a parallel career across the social divide, aiming to give less well off people better access to medical care, including children and pregnant women. It was a big contrast to the pompous traditionalist seen in the Infirmary. While still on the Infirmary staff, Ludlow was already combining that job and his own practice with taking charge of new and safer smallpox inoculations in a house at Barton Hill. (See pages 83-85.)

When he resigned from the Infirmary in 1774, Dr Ludlow did a lot more than just line his pockets from the private work. He lent his expertise, unpaid, to help set up a brand new type of community health centre, for patients unable to afford his fees as a doctor on call.

The Bristol Dispensary, initiated by Tabernacle Methodists, opened at the city end of Stokes Croft in 1775. It stood almost opposite where the Full Moon pub still is today, as the first in a network of about 20 dispensaries. They were gradually rolled out across Bristol during the nineteenth century.[121]

The original Bristol Dispensary, which opened in 1775, was located about where the traffic island and "Welcome to Stokes Croft" sign are now.

The design model for these early health centres combined a pharmacy, to dispense medication, with a waiting room and consulting rooms, for a doctor or surgeon to diagnose and treat their cash-strapped patients. Most of the dispensaries covered a particular district of the city, like Clifton, Redland or Bedminster. A few were set up to provide a specialist service, such as eye, ear or skin ailments, for the whole of Bristol. These were the forerunners, for example, of the Bristol Eye Hospital and the Children's Hospital.

The dispensary system, which developed more widely in Bristol than in most other cities, lasted until the start of the NHS in 1948. Dr Ludlow became the first lead physician at the original Bristol Dispensary. He organised and oversaw services there for about 25 years, until his retirement in the early 1800s. By 1807 its work was divided into two districts, north and south, and a second centre had opened in Bath Street. Both were eventually merged into a new central dispensary at Castle Green in 1853.

In Bristol the concept had originated with John Wesley and his own dispensary, which provided free medicine to the poor at the New Room chapel, built in 1739. (See Chapter 6.) However, that clinic folded after only a few years, due to funding and supply problems.

The Bristol Dispensary was another charity, based on subscriptions of about a guinea from each of its backers. They included the doctors it employed. In its first year there were 60 subscribers. By 1792 these had increased to 274.

Dr Ludlow had at least five other Quakers in his initial team. One was his younger medical colleague and friend John Till Adams. The medics were joined, as the Dispensary president and treasurer, by Joseph Beck of Frenchay Manor. He'd now become an extremely rich landowner. The diarist Sarah Champion Fox, who knew all of them like family, sat on the Dispensary committee, together with Beck's wife Mary and the chocolate maker Joseph Fry.

Dr Ludlow and a second physician/surgeon, Dr John Wright, played a key role in handling the most seriously ill cases. In one year, not specified in the committee's records, Ludlow attended 400 Dispensary patients himself and claimed over 150 women had been *"put to bed"* by its midwives. His aim was to expand capacity for delivering babies safely.[122]

In 1782 it was reported that in their first seven years the Dispensary team cared for a total of about 3,000 sick patients and delivered about 1,000 babies. By 1816 these numbers had increased massively, to a dozen times higher, but no figures were given for infant deaths.

There were strict rules, with a strongly moral tone, about what sort of people the Dispensary would accept for treatment. In 1792 its annual report stated: *"Only married women who can produce a certificate or other proof of their marriage can be proper objects of this charity as midwifery patients."*

The pregnant women had to apply to a female committee, at least a month in advance of when the baby was due. Any applicant with venereal disease was turned down. Generally, you were ineligible for treatment at the Dispensary if you could afford to pay, or if it was available at the nearby Bristol Infirmary. However, in those days the Infirmary made no provision for maternity patients or sick children.

The versatile John Till Adams was appointed at the Dispensary partly to work as a "man-midwife". Help in childbirth was traditionally provided by other women, with men only brought in for difficult labours and emergencies.

However, from around 1750 male surgeons and apothecaries started to become involved during regular births as well. They were now learning more about midwifery in new hospital training schemes.

Some women, especially the well off, preferred a man delivering their baby, on the assumption that he had more knowledge and technical expertise. For example, Till Adams supervised as man-midwife at the birth of William Fry, the druggist, in 1779. The mother was Hannah Fry (*nee* Dury) and the father John Plant Fry. Also present for the home birth in Dolphin Street was Hannah's sister Alice Bath (*nee* Dury), married to Shurmer Bath.[123]

However, using a man was a controversial choice. Opponents argued that male midwives did more harm than good by overreliance on their forceps and other instruments. They also said a woman's modesty was threatened by having her body exposed to men's gaze.

Man-Midwifery Dissected, a 1793 book by Samuel William Fores, challenged this invasion of a traditionally female sphere. His argument was illustrated in

The frontispiece of "Man-Midwifery Dissected" was a cartoon by Isaac Cruikshank. It depicts the male midwife as a hybrid figure, half man and half woman. The left half brandishes a lever to help pull the baby out. Behind him other large instruments hang, while on the shelves of his dispensary are love potions for the purpose of seduction. The right half is a woman in a cosy domestic setting, ready for a home birth.

the book with a striking cartoon.

Any patient, not just maternity, was accepted by the Bristol Dispensary only on the recommendation of a subscriber. The presence of so many Quakers on the charitable funding committees of the Dispensary and the Infirmary led to both these institutions identifying themselves more closely with public morality.

The most ground-breaking development at the Bristol Dispensary was the early introduction of cowpox vaccination against smallpox. By 1801, five years after Jenner's famous experiment on his gardener's son in Berkeley, the Dispensary began offering free vaccinations for children from poor families. They were carried out there twice a week, every Tuesday and Friday.[124]

Jenner had self-published his paper on vaccination just three years before, in 1798. A sceptical scientific establishment and general public in Britain had still not fully accepted the idea of using cowpox to immunise people against smallpox. Gillray drew his caricature of patients sprouting cow-like appendages in 1802. Jenner's method was being taken up faster abroad. It would be a further half century before the Compulsory Vaccination Act was passed by Parliament.

Bristol had some of the country's most enlightened and progressive minds in their attitude towards vaccination. Dr Abraham Ludlow, it seems, was a keen advocate. In 1801, now aged 64, the former terror of the Infirmary wards was nearing retirement but still active. In May that year, for instance, Sarah Champion Fox's Diary recorded her calling on Dr Ludlow to ask his opinion on a new medicine for her husband. In June he paid her a visit at home when she was *"very poorly"*. [125]

The evidence suggests that making free vaccinations available to children whose parents couldn't pay was initiated by Dr Ludlow and his colleagues. We know Ludlow had the necessary expertise, from the period in the 1760s when he gave new-style inoculations against smallpox at Barton Hill.

His old family connections with Jenner probably kept them in touch with each other. Dr Ludlow may have been one of those who requested supplies of the vaccine from his Berkeley colleague, in order to introduce it at the Bristol Dispensary. The new jabs were soon available more widely in the city.

In 1813 the Clifton Dispensary opened in Dowry Square, the first one serving just its own district of the Bristol area. Clifton's first annual report recorded a total of 160 vaccinations given there. From 1816 a new surgeon at the Infirmary, Nathaniel Smith, offered his own vaccination service. His outpatient appointment cards had a new message printed on them: *"Vaccinations every Tuesday at half-past Twelve"*.[126]

In 1838 six surgeons, at their own expense, opened the city's first public vaccination centre, the Bristol Vaccine Institution in St Augustine's Place. Parents had to pay sixpence for each child given the jab. This was refundable a week later if the measure proved successful and didn't need to be repeated.[127]

The Clifton Dispensary at 13 Dowry Square opened in 1813.

DOCTOR IN THE FAMILY

In contrast to his reputation for ludicrous posturing at the Infirmary, Dr Ludlow comes across in Sarah Champion Fox's Diary as kind, sociable and always available on call. It seems she first got to know him well from her visit

This sketch of Dr Abraham Ludlow is an illustration from the book 'A History of the Bristol Royal Infirmary', written by George Munro Smith

to the inoculation house at Barton Hill in 1768, when he was about 30. Two years later Sarah's sister Hetty and two other close female relatives all had bad coughs, or felt otherwise very weakened by illness. In April 1770 the Diary noted:

"It was thought necessary by A. Ludlow who was now become intimate in the family, that all should remove into the country. We accordingly engaged some lodgings at Henbury to which our family removed on the 28th May." [128]

Thereafter, Sarah mostly refers to him just as *"Dr L"*. She often mentions, in passing, invitations to dine in each other's homes. There's also an especially intriguing one-line entry in her Diary for July 1772:

"Drank tea with the Wesley family at Dr L." [129]

It's not clear whether this means John or Charles Wesley, or indeed both, plus Charles's wife Sally. But one would love to have been a fly on the wall at that tea party in Dr Ludlow's home in St Pauls. Unfortunately, Sarah's Diary gives no details at all. She knew both Wesley brothers, as did the doctor. At the time, Ludlow was in post at the Infirmary and may still have been giving smallpox inoculations at Barton Hill.

Tea with the Wesleys took place three years before the Bristol Dispensary was set up, inspired partly by John Wesley's earlier short-lived clinic at the New Room. Did they talk about free medical care for the poor? Or even John's passion for electrical therapy? Sadly, we'll never know.

Dr Ludlow married twice and, unusually for a Quaker, both his wives came from outside his religious community. They had Anglican backgrounds in Wiltshire.

With the first wife, Elizabeth Figgins from Devizes, Ludlow had two children, Harriet and Abraham. The boy was 11 when his mother died in 1790. Sarah Champion Fox's Diary reported that at her funeral in Bristol, at St

James's Church, *"the doctor grieved exceedingly after his wife".*[130] When Sarah next visited him two weeks later, he still *"seemed very poorly."*

In 1785, when his grown-up daughter Harriet was engaged to a mariner by the name of Captain James Walker, Dr Ludlow had bought Cote House on Durdham Down for the couple to live in after their wedding. He was later to die there in 1807, no doubt cared for by Harriet.

Dr Ludlow married his second wife in 1791, little more than a year after the death of his first. She was Elizabeth Gibbs (1735-1793), the rich widow of Gaisford Gibbs, a Wiltshire clothier. The family owned a country estate, Heywood, near Westbury. Elizabeth's father was another Westbury clothier, William Maltravers.

When he retired from the medical profession in the early 1800s, Dr Ludlow spent much of his time in Wiltshire, on the Heywood estate. It was now his, from that late and very rewarding second marriage to Elizabeth Gibbs. She had died in 1793, after only a couple of years with the doctor, leaving him a widower once again.

In his *History of the Bristol Royal Infirmary*, George Munro Smith gives this account of Dr Ludlow's final years, from an early twentieth century perspective:

"He endeared himself to his tenants [in Wiltshire] *by many acts of kindness. He frequently visited Bristol and saw his old comrades at the Infirmary, for whom he entertained no unfriendly feelings.*

"Some months before his death he noticed a swelling in his neck, which soon showed signs of malignancy. In those days – even more than now – there was no hope for such a condition, and this Ludlow knew only too well. He bore his sufferings with great fortitude, and died on July 15th, 1807, at the house of his married daughter, Mrs Walker [*Harriet*]*, at Redland."*[131]

This version of events tells only half the story. For decades Dr Ludlow had earned a vast salary from his medical practice in Bristol. Moving into Heywood on his retirement, he was worth an absolute fortune. Marriage to Elizabeth in 1791 brought Ludlow a Jacobean mansion, set in 25 acres of parkland with lawns, walled gardens, coach houses and other outbuildings. Her first husband Gaisford Gibbs had purchased the Heywood estate in 1789, then died two years later.

Heywood House, a Jacobean mansion near Westbury in Wiltshire, was rebuilt in the nineteenth century. Photo: from Ancestry website, courtesy of Carol Smith (Fitch family tree).

Following Elizabeth's own death in 1793, her daughter Susanna stood to inherit the estate. However, Abraham made certain that Heywood would stay in the Ludlow family, too, for the long term. His son, also Abraham, married Susanna in 1799, when he was only 19. The match guaranteed wealth and financial security for the Ludlows throughout the nineteenth century.[132]

Whether by accident or design, the canny doctor had found a way to make himself and his children even richer at the end of his life. Abraham Ludlow was 70 when he died in 1807. In an era of fundamental and lasting change for medical science, he made an important contribution. His work - especially in paving the way for, then introducing, Jenner's cowpox vaccination in Bristol - deserves far more recognition.

Ludlow may not always have appeared so, but he was progressive in approach and dedicated to improving healthcare for all his patients, from all walks of life. His rise to eminence came despite having a suspect qualification as a physician. To the resentment of some colleagues, he may never have been entitled to call himself Dr Ludlow M.D. However, in his career as a whole he achieved more than most – and also earned more.

CHAPTER 9
BODY SNATCHERS

As an epilogue to a remarkable life, let's go back half a century to an episode in Dr Ludlow's childhood. It's another story from the surgeon Richard Smith junior, whose biographical memoirs form the basis of the early twentieth century book *A History of the Bristol Royal Infirmary.* The anecdote, although highly amusing, is also quite gruesome. It may have been a traumatic early experience for the young Ludlow.

As mentioned earlier, there was no official medical school in Bristol until 1833, almost a century after the Infirmary opened in 1737. However, its surgeons had their own private students, who could also be their apprentices. They gave the young men lectures on Anatomy, of which dissection became an essential element. Fresh corpses were needed for this in ever increasing numbers, but demand far outstripped supply.

As a result, so-called body snatching was rife. It meant digging up newly buried corpses from graveyards and carrying them off for dissection.[133] One such grisly episode involved Abraham Ludlow senior. Like father like son, he was another extravagant character. Ludlow senior was a surgeon with a family home and successful practice at Castle Ditch in the city centre.

It was 1750. Two years later a new law would be passed, the Murder Act, to prevent the bodies of executed murderers being buried. Instead, they could be strung up on a gibbet, or legally given to medical science for dissection. This improved the supply of corpses for surgeons with an apprenticed student to teach, but there remained a shortage.

Abraham Ludlow senior heard about a notorious local criminal, known as "Long Jack", committing suicide by cutting his own throat. There was a custom, based on superstition, of burying suicides at a crossroads to stop them rising again. Ludlow set out one night to remove the body from its crossroads grave, in the direction of Kingswood.[134]

A watercolour drawing of Castle Ditch, Broad Weir & Ellbroad St Bridge, by Hugh O'Neill, 1821. This section of the River Frome had once formed part of the Castle moat. Broad Weir is the street on the left. It was an idealised scene. By the 1820s the river was a stinking cesspit, its pollution made worse by the construction of Bristol's Floating Harbour in 1809. During the 1700s the water was still tidal - and therefore self-cleansing, to some extent. (Image and information: courtesy of Bristol Culture, Bristol Museum & Art Gallery, M2882)

He took with him an apothecary, John Page, and his own son, the future Dr Ludlow, who was then only about 12. They dug up the body of "Long Jack", put it in a sack and tied it to their horse's back for the return journey. When the party arrived back at the city's Castle Gate, it was so late that the main entrance had closed for the night. They tried to get the laden horse through a side door, intended only for pedestrians.

According to the story told by Richard Smith junior, *"the body fell to the ground, and the porter, hearing a noise, came with his lantern and was not a little alarmed to see the legs of a man at the mouth of the sack. He was, however, persuaded to hold his tongue, and the cavalcade reached Mr Ludlow's house in safety. The body was placed upon a table in the back parlour, and the parties retired to rest themselves after their labours."*

Unfortunately, they forgot to lock the parlour door. When their maidservant came into the room in the morning, she was horrified to see the body of "Long Jack" lying on the table with his throat cut. She ran screaming into the road. News soon spread that there was a body in the house which had been "resurrected".

The Ludlows decided they must return the body that night and rebury it at the crossroads. It was lucky they did so. The next day a mob of angry local men went to check that Jack's corpse was in its grave, vowing revenge if not. They found it still there – and the Ludlow father and son, after a close shave, were off the hook. Otherwise the future career of 12-year-old Abraham could have been blighted very early on.

JOHNNY BALL LANE

Opposite the twenty-first century Children's Hospital, a narrow alleyway still plunges down in a series of doglegs to the city centre and quayside. It's called Johnny Ball Lane and, in the old days, it took you to the Infirmary's original burial ground a few steps from the top. Here they buried many of the ward patients who died, mainly paupers.

Think of the London slum graveyards in Dickens's *Bleak House* and you're probably close to the reality in Bristol a few decades earlier. Today the alleyway makes a picturesque stroll - in sunlight, anyway. Back then it was a grim spot,

made even grimmer by the threat of encountering body snatchers.

The Infirmary surgeon Richard Smith junior, known to his colleagues as Dick, was more than just a raconteur who enjoyed a lurid tale about stealing bodies from coffins. As a medical student he'd been one of the ringleaders - and quite proud of it.

In his biographical memoirs Smith recalls playing the role of *"Resurrection Men"*, with other students, to acquire corpses needed by the surgeons teaching them Anatomy. They got themselves into some *"awkward scrapes"*, as he puts it. One night Smith narrowly escaped being shot by soldiers guarding the Infirmary burial ground in Johnny Ball Lane. The young medics were opening coffins in the hospital's mortuary, removing the body and disguising their outrageous action afterwards.

"More than once, too, we substituted old sacks filled with rubbish, and...these were buried in due form...We had reduced this to so regular a system that we practised it two

years without suspicion. We procured a key of the dead-house [mortuary] *and provided ourselves with turn-screws, hammers, wrenching iron, nails, and everything likely to be wanted."*[135]

Nurses from the Infirmary and even some undertakers seem to have been bribed, so were complicit in the macabre raids. These often took place before the body had been laid to rest:

"The nurses and undertaker were allowed to take the ordinary course of laying out the subjects and securing the coffins. Funerals were generally ordered

Richard Smith junior, as portrayed in the frontispiece of 'A History of the Bristol Royal Infirmary'.

for five o'clock and whilst the family were at dinner we stole into the dead-house, removed anything we wanted, and then made all fast as before."

The surgeon who led their dissection classes, Francis Cheyne Bowles, was later smuggled into the mortuary, or *"dead-house"*. Smith describes it as a miserable subterranean *"coal hole lighted by a foot square iron grating"*, accessible through an opening from Lower Maudlin Street. The anatomical robbers spent many hours in these gruesome conditions, learning the structure of the human body from their teacher.

Bowles performed the clandestine dissections free of charge, motivated by a desire to pass on his zeal for Anatomy and *"insatiable thirst for knowledge"*.

By any moral standards this was shockingly cavalier behaviour. However, it's important to bear in mind that, at the time, taking a corpse didn't break the law. Only dissecting it afterwards was illegal. The Anatomy Act of 1832 eventually reversed this anomaly, to outlaw grave robberies but allow dissections.

The earlier legal change in 1752, giving surgeons access to the remains of executed murderers, had still failed to provide enough bodies for dissection. The surgeons were desperate for more. They felt the advancement of medical science outweighed their moral scruples and respect for the dead. In their view the end justified the means.

Members of the public expressed their fury in the press, both about the body snatching and the dissections. The Infirmary authorities, while very embarrassed, tried to avoid taking sides. However, after one complaint in March 1769, they were forced into disciplinary action against their medical students as a whole for *"removing the corpse from a coffin and substituting for burial a quantity of sand and wool"*. The students refused to apologise, but eventually backed down. A rule was introduced *"that the key of the dead-house be always in the custody of the* [Infirmary] *Apothecary"*.[136]

Body snatching for dissection had become commonplace in England during the eighteenth century. Usually, though, surgeons paid a gang known as "resurrection men" to do their dirty work for them. It was a widespread and lucrative business, with professional grave robbers in London charging as much as 10 or 20 guineas per corpse. They faced the risk of being attacked by family or friends of the deceased, guarding his or her burial spot.[137]

What seems different about Bristol is that a number of surgeons, and especially their young students, preferred DIY body snatching, rather than hiring someone else to do it. At the Infirmary they worked together in a highly organised way, often striking before the corpse had even been buried. Meanwhile, the medical authorities turned a blind eye to all this activity, unless the complaints got too loud to ignore.

The Infirmary students also made their own attempts, not always successful, to dig up bodies interred in the burial ground. When security was increased in Johnny Ball Lane by raising a high wall, the extra challenge only spurred them on. One such raid by the young medics, in March 1824, was reported to an Infirmary committee:

"They met at night at the Burying-Ground, but could not agree to act together. Some altercation arose, which gave an alarm and end to the attempt to get the body; but not to the hostile feelings of the two parties, which had to be appeased by some sort of pugilistic encounter some days after."

'Resurrection Men' by Thomas Rowlandson (1756 – 1827), late eighteenth century. In this satirical depiction two villainous grave robbers place the body of a newly buried woman into a sack, having removed it from the coffin. A skeleton assists by lighting their way.

MORE CONFESSIONS OF A BODY SNATCHER

Other graveyards across Bristol were also targeted by robbers. One dramatic example involved a burial ground near the Cathedral. In October 1819 a body was "snatched" from its coffin there. Two men, one with a sack on his back, were later seen entering a dissecting room in Lower College Street, above a greengrocer's shop. The shopkeeper told her neighbours and a crowd quickly gathered.[138]

Among the onlookers was a man whose wife had just died and been buried in St Augustine's churchyard. He at once went to the burial ground and found the grave had been opened. The man ran back to the dissecting room, climbed in through a window and found a sack containing his wife's body. Several of his friends joined him *"and a sharp contest ensued, but ultimately the corpse was carried off by the rightful owner. The Physician was pursued from the scene of the action by the mob, and narrowly escaped with his life."*

The *"Physician"* was believed by some in the know to be a surgeon called Thomas Earl, of 5 Lower College Street, but he wrote to the press angrily denying the allegation. A reward of 50 guineas was offered for information leading to the offenders being brought to justice.

FIFTY GUINEAS REWARD.

ST. AUGUSTINE's VESTRY ROOM,
Monday, 25th October, 1819.

WHEREAS on the Night of Friday last, or early on Saturday Morning, the Church-Yard of the Parish of St. Augustine was entered, and the Corpse of a Female which had been interred on the preceding Morning, was taken up and stolen therefrom, by some Persons unknown.

This is to give Notice, that a Reward of Fifty Guineas will be paid to any person who will give such information as may lead to the Conviction of the Offenders; the Vestry being determined to use every exertion to bring the parties who have been guilty of an act so abhorrent to the feelings of human nature, to justice.

The above Reward will be paid by Mr. Thos. Urch, Denmark-Street, the Churchwarden, on conviction of any one or more of the Offenders. An Accomplice making a discovery will receive the same Reward. OSBORNE & WARD, Vestry Clerks.

Bristol Mirror, Saturday 30 October 1819 (Image: British Newspaper Archive)

In February 1828 two grave robbers were caught in the churchyard at Brislington. They had tools with them, consisting of *"a shovel, a sack and a powerful turn-screw upon a novel construction, a packing needle and a coil of rope."*

The miscreants turned out to be a Dr Wallis, founder of a top Anatomy school in Bristol, and a fellow anatomist called Dr Riley. They were brought before a magistrate and fined £6 each, which they paid immediately. The incident seems to have done their careers no harm at all. Three weeks later the same magistrate proposed Dr Wallis for the post of physician at the Infirmary.

In November 1822 six medics also got off lightly after being apprehended outside Bedminster Church. Constables discovered them trying to remove a dead body from the churchyard. Five of the men were captured after a violent struggle, in which pistols and rapiers were drawn and blood spilt. They were sent for trial at the Somerset Quarter Sessions in Wells. The court bound them over to keep the peace, in the sum of £100, and took no further action.

The Bristol establishment, both legal and medical, tried to appear even-handed over body snatching, but in reality they sympathised with the surgeons. Francis Cheyne Bowles (1771-1807), the Anatomy teacher who surreptitiously dissected bodies stolen by his students, later gained promotion to the rank of physician at the Infirmary.

Bowles was born at Bradford-on-Avon in Wiltshire, the son of a wealthy gentleman barrister who moved to Bristol. The family were landed gentry with a long and distinguished history. An ancestor was knighted by Queen Elizabeth the First for his part in the capture and sacking of Cadiz in 1596. The young Francis trained as a surgeon at Guy's and St Thomas's Hospitals in London. He became known socially to his colleagues in Bristol, though, as plain "Frank Bowles" - a *bon vivant* who worked hard and also played hard.

Bowles was another curious mixture of dynamic constructive energy and frivolous vanity. In his memoirs Richard Smith describes his surgical mentor as *"fond of a beef-steak supper and a glass of punch, always ready for a midnight frolic and welcome at many festive gatherings."* He was, apparently, one of the *beaux* of the city and dressed in the elaborate style of an English buck during the French Revolution:

"His hair was fully pomatomed [brushed back from the forehead], *powdered and frizzed, and tied behind in a tail. His chin was buried in a large cravat...a fancy, figured, short waistcoat, a pair of high, leather, yellow breeches, reaching half way down the calf of his leg; blue silk stockings; a shoe which just covered his toes, surmounted with a large buckle, and false straps."*

This was the same man who also spent many hours in a secret underground hole, dissecting corpses "snatched" by his intrepid students, for the advancement of medical science.

In 1795 Bowles wrote a pamphlet on the ethics of body snatching, under the title *Thoughts on the Practice of Carrying off Bodies from Church Yards, etc., for Dissection*. This sought to justify it as a necessary evil, which must continue to be allowed by law: *"The safety of the public health should not be sacrificed to the weakness of our feelings."* [139]

A portrait of Dr Francis Cheyne Bowles, from 'A History of the Bristol Royal Infirmary'.

Bowles and a friend stood at the doors of the House of Commons with copies of the pamphlet, as MPs went in to debate a Bill that would have made the removal of bodies from graves a felony. The Bill was rejected, but the issue remained a legal grey area until 1832, when the Anatomy Act finally resolved it.

As a result of his dissipated youth, combined with a heavy workload and perhaps the fetid air of the mortuary, Bowles's career was cut tragically short. First he developed a chronic cough and a fever. Then his fragile health broke down completely, soon after he gained his physician post in 1806. Bowles died just a few months later, at the age of only 36.

In 1828 the difficulty of training surgeons in these circumstances led over 200 medics in the Bristol area to petition Parliament, demanding new legislation. The petition argued that a knowledge of the human body's structure, via dissection, was the basis of medicine and surgery, yet students could only acquire it by breaking the law. This was signed by almost all the Infirmary's staff. Their pressure undoubtedly influenced the passage of the Anatomy Act. From 1832 the body of a deceased person could be dissected lawfully, subject to their family's consent.

Richard Smith junior, the Infirmary's chief organiser of body snatching in his student days, prospered as a highly respected surgeon. In 1796 Richard became the third generation of his family to be appointed as a surgeon at the Infirmary. He carried on there for nearly half a century, until his death in 1843.

This operating table, with height adjusting mechanism, was donated by the surgeon Richard Smith junior to the Bristol Infirmary in 1786. Operations were carried out on it for the next 100 years. The table is now an exhibit at M Shed, Bristol. (Image: courtesy of Bristol Culture, Bristol Museum & Art Gallery.)

CHAPTER 10

BRISTOL INFIRMARY

The eighteenth century Infirmary building in Marlborough Street is still standing, having survived the bulldozers and all attempts by developers to have it pulled down. At the time of writing, in 2021, the old Infirmary was being converted into 62 smart residential apartments, with a cinema and private gym.[140]

Meanwhile, other buildings on the rest of the site behind it were all demolished, apart from the historic hospital chapel. They've made way for separate new accommodation, housing over 400 university students.

Bristol City Council approved the £39 million scheme in 2020, after turning down two earlier planning applications by Unite Students, owners of the whole site. There were hundreds of objections to a complete clearance and rebuild. A conservation area has since been extended to include the main

The front of the old Infirmary in spring 2021.

Demolition was in progress at the back of the old Infirmary in spring 2021, ready for purpose-built student accommodation. The hospital chapel, visible in the background, was saved.

building, so that it now has the added protection of Grade Two listed status.

When the original Infirmary opened as a charity institution in 1737, it was one of the first hospitals in England outside London. It initially admitted 34 patients – 17 men and 17 women – and had a similar number of visiting outpatients under the care of a physician or surgeon. Inpatients were expected to help clean the wards, which had wooden beds and were staffed by untrained low-paid nurses, working very long hours.[141]

There were strict rules, with patients made to wash their clothes before being admitted. They were forbidden *"to play cards or Dice or any Other Game within the Walls of the Infirmary, or smoak anywhere within Doors".* Nor were they allowed to *"swear, curse or give abusive Language".*

The hospital was managed by a matron, paid an annual salary of £15. The first matron, Ann Hughes, received about £100 a week from the Infirmary treasurer. Out of this she paid all the expenses for food and drink, plus the wages of nurses, servants, a residential in-house apothecary and his assistant.

The ward patients were given three meals a day, which varied according to which of four diets they were on. The *"Common Diet"* consisted of: for breakfast a pint of broth or *"milk pottage"*; for lunch ten ounces of beef or mutton on Sunday, Tuesday, Thursday and Saturday; on other days a pint of *"Rice-Milk or Pap"*; for supper a pint of broth or two ounces of cheese, on alternate nights. Twelve ounces of bread and three pints of small [weak] beer were given daily to each patient. A rule stipulated that *"no Greens of any kind"* should be provided in their meals.

In 1749 the Infirmary had 76 beds available. Already there was overcrowding and a cash shortage. That year almost 200 patients had to be turned away and lodged in nearby houses. By 1755 the number of beds had doubled to 150 to meet ever increasing demand.[142]

VOTE FOR LUDLOW!

Funding came from the Infirmary's well off subscribers, who were each expected to contribute at least one or two guineas a year. A committee of 12 met twice a week to decide which patients to admit. Subscribers also elected the matron and all the senior medical staff – four surgeons and two physicians at first, soon increasing to five of each – in a ballot. Two guineas a year guaranteed you a vote as a member of the Board of Trustees.

These elections could become as hard fought and heated as a political contest. Each candidate had supporters who canvassed for votes on their behalf, and public feeling often ran high. When Abraham Ludlow competed with a rival, Thomas Skone, for a surgeon's post in 1767, it ended in a dead heat.[143]

This true story was another of those saved for posterity by Richard Smith junior. It's reminiscent of the hilariously satirical episode in Dickens's early novel *The Pickwick Papers*, about rivalry and skulduggery at a parliamentary election in the fictional constituency of "Eatanswill".

The Infirmary election took place in a packed room at the city's Merchant Tailors' Hall. It was expected to be close and everyone waited in great excitement for the outcome. All 293 votes, on bits of paper, were put into hats, one for each candidate. The chairman, local grandee Sir Abraham Elton, did the counting himself and announced the result: for Mr Skone 147, for Mr Ludlow 146. He added: *"Gentlemen, I am by no means certain that I am correct."*

The friends of Ludlow shouted: *"A scrutiny! A scrutiny! Tell the votes again,"* while the rest cheered and shouted *"Victory! Victory!"* Eventually there was a careful recount, before another declaration: Mr Ludlow 147, Mr Skone 146!

In the words of Richard Smith junior: *"This announcement led to a scene of tumult, and it looked very much like there was going to be a free fight with canes and sticks. Sir Abraham with great difficulty persuaded the meeting to allow a fresh count to be made by two people.*

"This was scarcely agreed to when a young friend of Mr Skone made an attempt to toss a vote privately into his hat, which being perceived on the other side, his example was imitated and in a second or two more papers were thrown into the other hat."

In the ensuing chaos both hats were tipped over and the papers scattered on the floor. It became impossible to declare a winner. Some called for a fresh election, others for a postponement, while a third party clamoured for both men to be elected. It was eventually decided to take that last option and appoint both candidates to the position of surgeon.

This fiasco of an election is easily satirised, but there's also a serious point. Gaining a position at the Infirmary had very little to do with your medical or surgical skills – and everything to do with who you knew among Bristol's "great and the good". The subscribers were generally a conservative lot, with a big 'C' as well as a small one. They suspected any religious dissenters, including Quakers, of being political radicals - and therefore unsuitable for the Infirmary.

Having a prominent Quaker, like a Harford or Champion, as treasurer or president helped to redress the balance somewhat, but prejudice against dissenters still persisted. It could be extra difficult for a Quaker to further his hospital career, which may explain Dr Ludlow's bumpy ride at the Infirmary.

Being a Quaker certainly counted against Ludlow's younger colleague and friend Joseph Metford (1755-1833). Metford became an Infirmary surgeon in 1783, but only after three previous applications for a post had been turned down. This was despite the young man having proven skills as a surgical apprentice at the Infirmary. He was even allowed to amputate someone's leg

The original Bristol Infirmary as it was in 1765, before a rebuild from the 1780s onwards. Eventually, during the twentieth century, the hospital was moved to new sites on the opposite side of Upper Maudlin Street.

at the tender age of 17.

George Munro Smith, the author of *A History of the Bristol Royal Infirmary*, had no doubt that Metford fell victim to religious and political discrimination under Tory government rule:

"He failed chiefly because he was a Quaker and a Whig. It was thought that he owed his success at his fourth canvass in great measure to the fact that the Rockingham Administration of 1782, and the coalition of Mr [Charles James] Fox with Lord North, had for a time shown the public the folly of voting for, or against, a man merely on account of his religious or political opinions." [144]

VOTES FOR WOMEN

When Dr Abraham Ludlow resigned from the Infirmary in December 1774, the election to replace him as a surgeon was the first to allow a woman the right to vote. It happened on the initiative of a Miss Elton, said to be *"a maiden lady of good family, living in some style in Orchard Street. She was descended from the Eltons of Stapleton, was stout of person, an admirer of the Stage and a patroness of Genius."* [145]

Richard Smith senior won the ballot at the Guildhall in Broad Street by a large majority among 580 subscribers, of whom 70 were female. His son later wrote an amusing but patronising account of the event:

"No-one had ever heard, or even dreamed of such a thing as a Lady's giving a vote

The current site of the Grand Hotel in Broad Street is where the White Lion Hotel stood in 1774. The Infirmary's 70 female subscribers gathered there to vote in an election for a new surgeon, taking place at the Guildhall (visible on the left in the photo). However, only the women's leader got to cast her ballot. In the end, the men wouldn't allow the rest of them to participate.

for a Surgeon to the Infirmary, but nevertheless a Miss Elton suggested the Scheme and Mr Smith very readily adopted the plan. A considerable number of ladies were, with great secrecy, collected at the White Lion, ready to vote if needful, and by way of trying the question, Miss Elton insisted on giving her vote. The adverse party were entirely surprised and endeavoured by urging the want of precedent to disqualify the suffrage. Miss Elton, however, contended that the law was too clear to be shaken; it was 'that every person paying two guineas per annum shall become a Trustee and that all Trustees have votes'. After much altercation the vote was accepted and the lady retired in triumph to marshal her amazons. It appearing however that there was no real doubt respecting the issue, Mr Smith went to thank the ladies for their kind attentions, but declined giving them trouble merely to swell a majority."

The spirited woman invited to *"marshal her amazons"* at the White Lion Inn was, in fact, called Mary Elton. Her name appears in *Sketchley's Bristol Directory of 1775,* giving her address as 4 Orchard Street. It's worth noting that Miss Elton was, as it turned out, the only one among the 70 women subscribers who got to cast a vote. The men decided ultimately that because Smith senior had a comfortable winning margin without them, female suffrage wasn't necessary after all. Richard Smith senior favoured votes for women only if they made the difference between him winning and losing. We'll never know how significant this event might have proved for women if the contest had been close.

MURDER OF A PHYSICIAN

One of the first two physicians (university-qualified doctors) appointed at the Infirmary in 1737 was Dr William Logan. He was another Quaker who made his imposing presence felt on the wards by dressing to look the part. This is how Dr Logan always presented himself in public, according to a contemporary's description:

"He was a strict observer of professional costume, and never stirred abroad, or was visible at home, unless in full dress, i.e. his head covered by the immense flowing wig of George the Second's time, a red roquelaure [red cloak] *hanging down from his shoulders to his heels, his wrist graced with a gold-headed cane, and his side furnished with a long French rapier."* [146]

However, even the rapier couldn't save Dr Logan from a terrible lingering death. In 1747 he was deliberately poisoned with arsenic by one of his servants. Dr Logan and his wife employed a lad called William Nicholas as a domestic servant in their home at Castle Green. Nicholas harboured a grudge against them, accusing the couple of being stingy with his wages. He confessed later that the poisoning idea came to him when sitting opposite Mrs Logan at a Quaker religious meeting. [147]

One Sunday Nicholas activated a planned strategy, after obtaining a quantity of arsenic. He awaited the right opportunity, when his fellow servant was away, and dropped it into the Logans' breakfast chocolate. The couple both fell violently ill and Mrs Logan died a few months later. Her husband survived for 10 years, but his shattered health never recovered. Dr Logan also eventually died, from the long-term effects of the poison, in 1757.

Meanwhile, their servant had been arrested soon after the crime and faced trial at the Guildhall Assizes. William Nicholas was convicted of murder on 6 April 1748 and sentenced to death. He was hanged from the gallows at the top of St Michael's Hill on 22 April. The next day a local newspaper, the *Oracle County Advertiser*, published a report on the execution, which had been carried out at about one o'clock in the afternoon.

The young man *"behaved very Penitent, desiring all young Persons to take Warning by him, declaring at the same Time that what he did was not with Intent to commit murder. He ty'd his Handkerchief over his face and ask'd the Hangman for his Cap, which he had just before put in his Waistcoat Pocket. After he was cut down, his Body was delivered to his Friends, in order for Interment."* [148]

By contrast a dragoon soldier, sentenced to death at the same Assizes for the murder of a tobacco cutter, was reprieved from the hangman's noose. The judge also ordered a woman guilty of a lesser crime to be *"burnt in the hand"* and a man to be *"whipped publickly"*.

I've been unable to confirm for sure that Dr Logan was related to a Quaker from America, known as *"William Logan of Philadelphia"*. The latter met Sarah Champion Fox on a visit to Bristol in September 1761. He's mentioned briefly in her Diary as *"a very agreeable man, in the opinion of our sex especially"*. Sarah recorded having tea with William Logan of Philadelphia, her aunt and a cousin. It took place four years after Dr Logan's death, while Sarah was still in her teens. [149]

It's possible the two Logans came from different families and had the same name by complete coincidence. However, it's far more likely the poisoned Dr Logan was also American, was father, uncle or older brother of the other, and had crossed the Atlantic to settle in Bristol.

Now the story gets even more complicated. There was also a link between the Logan family and the founder of Pennsylvania, William Penn. Back in the 1690s someone by the name of James Logan had succeeded his Irish Quaker father as schoolmaster at the Friars Meeting House in Bristol. In 1699 James was made William Penn's secretary and travelled with him to Pennsylvania, eventually becoming Deputy Governor of the new colony. [150]

James Logan had a grandson, William, who was sent back to England as an apprentice to Dr Henry Portsmouth in Basingstoke. This was the same doctor who'd trained a young Joseph Fry, and whose eldest daughter Anna had married Joseph.

During his apprenticeship William Logan made a "runaway match" with one of Dr Portsmouth's other daughters, called Sarah.[151] They eloped to London, married at an Anglican church there in 1769 and sailed to America. The couple set up home in Philadelphia and had a baby, but William died soon afterwards. He was given a Quaker burial in the American city.

In 1772 William's widow obtained a certificate from Philadelphia Quakers Monthly Meeting for a return to England with her infant son, William Portsmouth Logan. On a very stormy Atlantic crossing Sarah was accompanied by the ubiquitous druggist and doctor John Till Adams. He was returning from his own voyage to America and about to start wooing Ann Fry.

If it were the plot for a novel, we'd dismiss this web of interconnections as too far-fetched. However, in their small nonconformist community, where everyone knew each other and rallied round any honest Quaker needing help, it seems fact could be stranger than fiction.

CHAPTER 11
MADHOUSE DOCTOR

Dr Edward Long Fox (1761-1835) was yet another Quaker physician who stood out from the crowd. He had more impact at national level than any of our other chosen medics, apart from Edward Jenner. Fox did so through his work as a pioneering psychiatrist, or "madhouse doctor".

Dr Fox has featured briefly already, in Chapter 3. He dabbled in animal magnetism, otherwise known as mesmerism, during unsuccessful experimental treatment on his patients at the Bristol Infirmary in the late 1780s.

He belonged to the same well-to-do family from Devon and Cornwall as Charles Fox, the Plymouth banker who married Sarah Champion in 1790. Edward was the son of Joseph Fox, an apothecary and surgeon in Falmouth, where both men initially worked together in general practice. Edward then studied medicine at Edinburgh University, before practising in Plymouth as a qualified physician from 1784.[152]

The doctor became part of Sarah Champion Fox's extended family circle on her travels to the far South West, then in Bristol, where he lived as her neighbour at Castle Green. He joined the Infirmary's senior staff in 1786, aged only 25, and remained in his post there for the next 30 years as a very active member of the team.[153]

Dr Fox soon also built up an enormous private medical practice. He inherited the patient list of his illustrious fellow Quaker, Dr John Till Adams, who'd died recently. At the same time, Fox invested in various commercial projects across the region, including new canals and public utilities. His business flair with these investments, in addition to the income from private medicine, made him rich enough to move from Castle Green in 1793 to live in Queen Square, alongside some of the city's wealthiest merchants.

Meanwhile, Dr Fox gained some notoriety from his campaigning for political causes, to go with his status as a religious dissenter. In 1788 he was one of

Portrait drawing of Dr Edward Long Fox by an unknown artist.

five Quakers among the 20 original members of a Bristol committee petitioning parliament to abolish the transatlantic slave trade.[154]

In October 1793 Dr Fox called a public meeting in protest at the killing of at least 11 people by soldiers in the city centre. The militia had been summoned to quell serious rioting over an increase in the tolls on Bristol Bridge. They fired on a large mob and charged at them with fixed bayonets. Dr Fox tended some of the 45 victims left injured in the mayhem.[155]

There was a febrile atmosphere across Britain in the aftermath of the French Revolution, amid nervousness that its violent anarchy might spread to Bristol and other urban areas this side of the Channel. Dr Fox was branded a Jacobin, or revolutionary sympathiser, by some of the local ruling elite. He even had stones hurled at his carriage as it drove along the city's streets.

In 1795, with Britain and France gearing up for the Napoleonic Wars, he again fell foul of the Bristol establishment. Dr Fox chaired a large public meeting in support of a peace treaty with France, and found himself accused of deliberately inflaming passions and inciting the populace to revolt.

Fox was strongly defended in print by a young Samuel Taylor Coleridge. The poet, who lived in Bristol at the time, had got involved in the city's politics as a public lecturer and radical campaigning journalist. However, Coleridge also had a growing addiction to opium, a chaotic family life and a chronic shortage of money. In return for the poet's written support, Dr Fox became a patron for Coleridge, making a donation of £50.[156]

SHEER LUNACY

It was in his pioneering work as a psychiatrist that Edward Long Fox really made his mark and created a lasting legacy. He did start a revolution – not to overthrow the state, but to improve the treatment of mental illness.

Dr Fox was a bold medical entrepreneur, with a knack of doing the right thing for his patients while also making a handsome profit. By 1799 he'd saved enough capital from his private practice and investments to embark on the main venture of his career. The doctor had already been running a successful "lunatic asylum", at Cleve Hill in Downend, for seven years. However, the building's structural layout was unsuitable for the changes he wanted.

He now bought 300 acres of common land for £4,000 at Brislington, a village near Bristol on the way to Bath, and made plans to build his own state-of-the-art institution. Dr Fox believed in the restorative power of fresh air and nature, in a familiar domestic environment, for treating "insanity" – or, in modern parlance, mental illness.[157]

In the "Age of Enlightenment", so-called "lunatics" were still often cruelly locked up, and even chained, like wild animals that must be tamed. Dr Fox led a new generation of reformers who favoured a kinder and more humane regime, based on the premise that madness was curable. His innovative approach involved categorising patients according to their social class, gender and mental state. Each group would live separately from the rest – so that a distressed gentleman, for example, never had to mix with his social inferiors.

Dr Fox designed every last detail of Brislington House to turn these principles into reality. It was one of Britain's first purpose-built asylums and became the model for a network of new mental health institutions, in both the public and private sectors, during the nineteenth century,

When Brislington House finally opened in 1806, the cost of building and equipping it totalled an enormous £35,000, all from Dr Fox's own savings. That would be over three million today. A few of the 100 or so residential places were reserved for "pauper lunatics", paid for out of parish funds. However, the new asylum was geared mainly towards a well off and fee-paying clientele.

It stood surrounded by extensive landscaped gardens and pleasure grounds, just off the main road from prosperous Bristol to fashionable Bath. Part of the site is occupied now by St Brendan's Sixth Form College. As Leonard Smith observed in a profile of Dr Fox for the *History of Psychiatry* in 2008:

"*Brislington House could hardly have been more favourably located for attracting custom from the aristocracy, gentry and moneyed middle classes.*" [158]

BRISLINGTON HOUSE ASYLUM

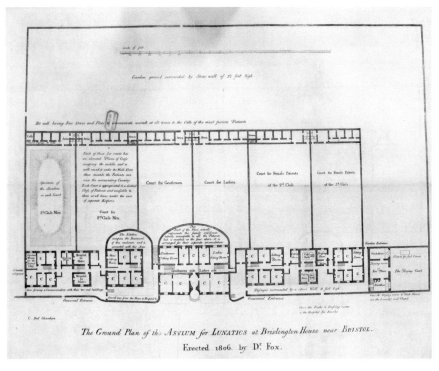

Ground plan for Brislington House, published in about 1809. (Image: The National Archives, MPI 1/332/1)

Dr Fox's big idea was that for recovery to take place, mental health patients must be removed from their family and friends, who may have caused their breakdown. Instead, they should be placed in an institution under specialist care. Here, as much as possible, their environment should replicate the home surroundings they were used to and where they felt comfortable. [159]

He divided his patients into three social classes, reflecting each level of Georgian society as a whole, and built his asylum so that each rank lived

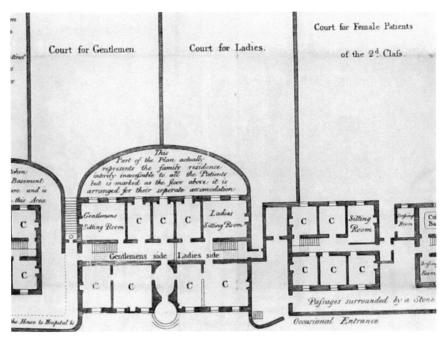

A section of the 1809 ground plan, showing how patients were separated by their social class and sex.

separately from the other two. Men were also separated from women, and patients with the worst symptoms kept apart from the milder cases.

An early ground plan shows how this segregation was achieved by Fox's unique design. The asylum comprised a row of seven detached houses, spaced out evenly in a symmetrical pattern. The central house was the largest and most expensive, for the upper class only. It was divided into two sections, one for gentlemen and the other for ladies. Each had its own staircase and communal sitting room, and everyone was given an individual bedroom. Dr Fox moved into this building, too, with his large family. He married twice and had 15 daughters and eight sons. That's 23 children in all!

Three more single-sex houses were built on each side of the central building, again separated into accommodation for patients deemed second class and, furthest along, third class. In between were those with physical ailments as well as mental ill health. Each building also had separate courtyards, for exercise and fresh air, with an elevated grassy mound in the middle where patients could view the surrounding countryside. But the yards also incorporated 12-feet-high walls to prevent escape.

Engraving of house and garden from 'History and Present State of Brislington House', by Francis and Charles Fox, 1836. (Image: Wellcome Library. Reproduced under Creative Commons Attribution only licence *CC BY* 4.0)

Dr Fox used materials in the construction to reduce the fire risk, like iron instead of wood in doors, joists and window frames. Where possible, too, measures were put in place to deter suicide, including low doorways, high windows and tables and chairs secured to the floor. Hot and cold plunge baths were provided for therapeutic treatment, also a chapel for regular Church of England services. Fox made no attempt to impose his own beliefs as a nonconformist, and therefore minority, Quaker, but he considered religion important for restoring mental equilibrium.

The patients also had plenty of outdoor activities and amusements at their disposal in the grounds. For the upper crust there were greyhounds, tame fowls, pheasants and doves. The lower orders could do gardening, farm work or odd jobs around the estate, and play cricket or football. They even had a bowling green. There was also access to a scenic wooded walkway along a steep cliff top, presumably well fenced, high above the River Avon.

Dr Fox employed a high ratio of staff, or *"keepers"*. He told them to use a minimum of coercion and force. Nevertheless, the *"most furious"* patients were sometimes put under restraint in their isolation *"cells"*, which were heated by flues.

The innovations and standard of care drew an overwhelmingly favourable response. A parliamentary report in 1815 ranked Brislington House at number one in a list of private "madhouses" to emulate. In the public sector a small network of asylums, funded by taxation, had been evolving since the mid 1700s. The first was St Luke's in London, followed by others in some provincial cities, including Manchester, York, Liverpool and Exeter.

In the early nineteenth century, designs for the first county asylums, then subsequent ones, were modelled on Dr Fox's establishment. Their planners and managers took advice directly from him. They had a lot to improve on.

BEDLAM

The 1815 report, singling out Brislington House for high praise, was by a Quaker MP, Edward Wakefield. He visited a range of private and public asylums to inspect and compare the conditions. The MP's report was for the parliamentary Select Committee on Madhouses in England. He witnessed some real-life horror stories of inmates being subjected to barbaric treatment, which nowadays we'd call torture.[160]

In his testimony to the Committee, Edward Wakefield described what he saw at the oldest and worst institution, Bethlem Hospital in London. It was nicknamed "Bedlam" - so notorious that it's passed into the English language as a byword for scenes of terrifying madness and uproar. The MP visited the women's galleries first:

"One of the side rooms contained about ten patients, each chained by one arm or leg to the wall; the chain allowing them merely to stand up by the bench or form fixed to the wall, or to sit down on it. The nakedness of each patient was covered by a blanket-gown only...the feet even were naked. One female...stated that she had been a teacher of languages; the keepers described her as a very accomplished lady, speaker of several languages, and corroborated her account of herself. The Committee can hardly imagine a human being in a more degraded and brutalizing situation than that in which I found this female, who held a coherent conversation with us, and was of course fully sensible of the mental and bodily condition of those wretched beings, who, equally without clothing, were closely chained to the same wall with herself."

Wakefield found conditions in the men's wing to be equally barbaric:

'A Rake's Progress VIII: The Madhouse', 1734, by William Hogarth (Photo: © Sir John Soane's Museum, London)

In the side room, six patients were chained close to the wall, five handcuffed, and one locked to the wall by the right arm, as well as by the right leg; he was very noisy; all were naked, except as to the blanket gown or a small rug on the shoulders, and without shoes; one complained much of the coldness of his feet...The patients in this room, except the noisy one, and the poor lad with cold feet, who was lucid when we saw him, were dreadful idiots; their nakedness and their mode of confinement gave this room the complete appearance of a dog kennel...Whilst [we were] looking at some of the bed-lying patients, a man arose naked from his bed, and had deliberately and quietly walked a few paces from his cell door along the gallery; he was instantly seized by the keepers, thrown into his bed and leg-locked, without enquiry or observation: chains are universally substituted for the strait-waistcoat."

In stark contrast to the horror of Bedlam, Edward Wakefield's observations on Brislington House were very positive:

"I did not see above two or three patients even in strait waistcoat, none

Long Fox Manor, formerly Brislington House, is now divided into private apartments.
(Photo: reproduced under Creative Commons licence CC BY SA 3.0)

in chains. The laundry is converted into a chapel on a Sunday, where service is regularly performed...There is a separate bedroom to each patient, all well ventilated, whitewashed, and cleaned: the patients tranquil, without coercion, but not allowed to remain in bed."

The Committee's findings marked a turning point in attitudes towards treatment of madness, even though no legislation followed until 13 years later. Public opinion, which had once looked on madness as a spectator sport, swung decisively behind regulation and reform.[161]

Edward Wakefield's very shocking account of Bedlam brings the regime at Brislington House into true perspective for our modern eyes. It helps us understand why Dr Fox's asylum, based on the rigid class structure of Georgian England, was seen as enlightened and progressive. It was certainly no prescription for social mobility. However, our twenty-first century aim to make Britain less dominated by class wasn't shared back then. Any talk of a more flexible and less hierarchical society would have been regarded by the ruling elite, and most of the public, as dangerous revolutionary propaganda.

There was a contradiction between Dr Fox's radical stance in politics -

battling for justice for the downtrodden - and his recreation of the class status quo at Brislington House. In fact, though, he was among the first to recognise that treating mental disorders required not brutal confinement but a humane, calm and safe environment, fostering self-discipline and strong moral values. To achieve this in an asylum, you had to embrace the class structure of the outside world, not reject it.

In 1816 Fox resigned from his other job, as a physician at the Bristol Infirmary, after 30 years there, to focus more on running his asylum. He eventually handed over the asylum management to two of his numerous sons, Drs Francis and Charles Fox, in 1829. Brislington House remained in the family, as a mental health institution, until the Second World War.

It went on to become a nurses' home until the 1980s, then a care home for the elderly, before being converted into private apartments in the early noughties. The original row of detached houses was joined together, and the front altered, in the mid nineteenth century. Brislington House now has a different name, Long Fox Manor, in memory of its illustrious founder. Unfortunately, there's no public access to see it.

CHAPTER 12

POLAR ATTRACTION

The dawning of a new century found Sarah Champion Fox at a low ebb. The diarist was nearing her sixtieth birthday and in declining health. She'd always assiduously called on her family and friends when they fell ill. The Diary is full of these visits, which in her Quaker way she considered a mixture of duty and pleasure. Now an ageing Sarah, increasingly, needed to consult Dr Ludlow or Dr Fox on her own painful rheumatism and other ailments.

Sarah was still very active, but on a downward path. More and more of her old Bristol friends (in both the personal and Quaker sense) were being "removed" to the burial grounds. In July 1800 she lost one of her favourites, Shurmer Bath, who'd been ill for several years. In August 1801 her husband Charles died, with Sarah at his bedside, on a visit to his family in Plymouth.

In her final Diary entry for 1801, on 13 December, Sarah gives us this brief sad reflection on her state of health and mind, and whether she can go on writing about everyday life:

"Time has made & seems making such rapid inroads in my mortal part the last three years, that I am apprehensive even this favourite employment of journalizing must give way." [162]

In June 1802 Sarah commented on an important new friendship, which was to bring her much comfort in her remaining years. It was with an American Quaker physician, Dr Thomas Pole, and his family. She wrote on 2 June:

"The next day we had the company [at 14 St James Square] *of Dr Pole, his valuable wife, with two sons & three daughters. They appeared to be a family of love, & individually pleasing - the eldest a fine young man. I hope to be favoured with a more intimate knowledge of E. Pole,* [Elizabeth] *as well as her worthy husband."* [163]

Thomas Pole (1753-1829) had joined the throng of distinguished Bristol doctors from a Quaker background – in his case in Philadelphia. What made him different from most of the Champion Fox social crowd was that he settled

in Bristol in middle age. By this time he'd already built an international reputation in the new field of obstetrics.

The American had other strings to his bow. He combined his medical work with preaching far and wide as a Quaker minister and with painting exquisite watercolours of houses, or monotint portraits and silhouettes of his family and friends. These soon included Sarah. After 20 strenuous years in London, Dr Pole moved to Bristol for a quieter life. He heard the newly widowed Sarah Champion Fox was selling her house, 14 St

Silhouette of Sarah Champion Fox by Dr Thomas Pole, circa 1806. (Image: part of an illustration from a posthumous biography of Dr Pole, written by his great-grandson)

James Square, and bought it from her as the Pole family home.[164]

The diarist wanted somewhere smaller for her old age, as she had explained in an entry the previous year, in August 1801:

"The beginning of this month I went to see a small house in Brunswick Square, I had been induced to purchase, after, I hope, due consideration. I thought a smaller abode would add to my comfort and lessen my cares if not expenses."[165]

The Poles had been frequent visitors to Bristol throughout their two decades living in London. Thomas's future wife, Elizabeth Barrett, was already one of Sarah's acquaintances in Cheltenham, known to her as Betsy, when the couple married in 1784. Later, in July 1796, Sarah was in attendance at the Quakers Friars Meeting House when Dr Pole came to preach twice on the same day. He was *"mostly addressing servants and those in what are called inferior stations."* She was impressed by his performance as a preaching minister:

"At both [meetings] I heard Thos Pole, who appeared greatly enlarged in his gift since I heard him some years ago. He also appeared greatly improved in person by being increased in size."[166]

In May 1802, when she was poorly and had Thomas staying as her lodger, Sarah needed his skills as a family doctor more than his powers of oratory:

"I found myself very unwell. I was obliged to return to bed not being able to sit up, and was soon reduced to a considerable state of weakness. I was carefully attended to by my kind Doctor, whose capacity, as I believed, of sympathising with the mind (though no words were dropped expressive of it,) as well as bodily infirmities was truly comfortable to me." [167]

CHILDBIRTH DOCTOR

Thomas Pole's family origins lay in the Somerset villages of Wiveliscombe and Milverton. His father John Pole (1705-1755) was a Quaker who started a tailoring business, but ran up debts and emigrated to Burlington, New Jersey, to avoid jail. He eventually paid off his creditors, married a local girl and moved to Philadelphia. Thomas was born there in 1753, the youngest child of four. Both parents died when he was small. Much of Thomas's life story has come down to us from a short biography by his great-grandson, Edmund Tolson Wedmore, published in 1908.[168]

As a boy Thomas was looked after by a family guardian, and briefly went off the rails when he *"yielded to sinful gratifications"*. He soon saw the light, reformed and became a Quaker minister when still only 19. In 1775 Thomas Pole sailed to England to see his relatives and set off on a nationwide preaching tour of Friends' meeting houses. He travelled 6,000 miles around England and Wales, mostly on horseback, over the next couple of years.

He never returned to America. Instead, the young Thomas now devoted himself to medicine. He became apprenticed to a surgeon and apothecary in Maidenhead, Berkshire, before going to Falmouth to assist Dr Joseph Fox in general practice. Joseph was the father of Bristol's mental health pioneer, Dr Edward Long Fox (profiled in Chapter 11). Theirs was another example of Quaker links far and wide boosting a career in medicine.

In the early 1780s Dr Pole went to live in London, where he became qualified in midwifery. He built up his own large practice, specialising in the traditionally female role of delivering babies. The American man-midwife also delivered lectures to his students every morning on the new childbirth science of obstetrics. These lectures, which took place in Dr Pole's surgery premises between St Thomas's Hospital and Guy's, were illustrated with his

Portrait of Dr Thomas Pole by Nathan Cooper Branwhite (date unknown).

own anatomical drawings.

His work soon drew admiring attention from the medical establishment, despite his parallel career as a Quaker minister. Thomas Pole was admitted to the Company of Surgeons in London; became elected a member of the American Philosophical Society, which had Benjamin Franklin as president at the time; and gained a medical degree from St Andrews University to qualify as a physician.

All the while, Dr Pole continued his itinerant preaching duties for the Society of Friends. This took him to Bristol and other Quaker meeting houses across the country, always carrying his drawing materials with him.

Inevitably, this constant overworking took its toll on his own health, which broke down in 1801. Dr Pole left the capital with Betsy for two months of complete rest and therapeutic spa treatment. He took the waters in Betsy's home town, Cheltenham. There his therapy was supervised by Dr Edward Jenner, who by then had qualified as a consulting physician.

Thomas followed this up with a three-week stay in Bath, before returning to London refreshed. Despite his rare vacation, Dr Pole again found himself under intolerable pressure from the demands of midwifery, preparing daily lectures, preaching, and collecting specimens for his anatomical museum. The family decided on a complete change as the only way forward.

Dr Pole moved into Sarah's old house at 14 St James Square, Bristol, with his wife and their four surviving children. Here the newcomer opted for a still heavy, but less stressful, workload and a bit more spare time for his art.

The Poles' new life in Bristol got off to an inauspicious start, with a family tragedy soon after their arrival. Their eldest son John, the one described in Sarah's Diary as a *"fine young man"*, was never able to fulfil some early promise.

In London John had been one of his father's medical pupils, assisting in the surgery and with his lectures. In November 1803 he died from typhoid, when still only 18 years old.

By now Dr Pole was back in the thick of it, with a rapidly expanding Bristol medical practice and with childbirth still his specialty. He also began a new series of public lectures, this time covering a whole range of science subjects. They were designed for wider audiences and intended as a true reflection of the Enlightenment.

Portrait of Elizabeth Pole ("Betsy") as a young woman, by her husband Dr Thomas Pole. Watercolour drawing from a private collection.

His particular aim was to make the lectures appeal to women as well as men. The course had an overall title - *The Economy of Nature* - and included Surgery, Botany, Mineralogy, Chemistry, Physics, the use of Globes, Midwifery, Optics and Astronomy. With his usual tongue-in-cheek humour, the Infirmary chronicler Richard Smith labelled Dr Pole *"Professor of Things in General"*.[169]

The lectures were given in Dr Pole's own house, 14 St James Square. He charged a fee of four guineas for the whole course, or you could pay two shillings and six pence for a single lecture on the topic that interested you most. Again he provided illustrations of the subject matter from his own drawings.

We have no information on whether Sarah or Betsy enrolled, but the lectures were certainly open to them. Dr Pole issued a prospectus in 1802, stating that his courses in General Science would be adapted to people of either sex. His great-grandson Edmund Tolson Wedmore put it like this in his biography, written a century later: *"He deemed women to have been too much excluded from opportunities of scientific improvement."*[170]

It's tempting to wonder if those attending the lectures were served drinks or snacks by the Poles' aged family retainer, Mary Daniel. Known by all as

The Pole family's servant, Mary Daniel ("Molly") in the hallway of their home, 14 St James Square.
Drawing by her long-standing employer Dr Thomas Pole, circa 1820s.
(Image: illustration from a biography of Dr Pole, written by his great-grandson.)

A view of the entrance to 14 St James Square from York Street, with two gardeners at work. Colour drawing on paper by Dr Thomas Pole. (Image: courtesy of Bristol Culture, Bristol Museum & Art Gallery, ref K4358)

"Molly", she worked for the Pole family as their live-in servant for three decades. She looked after all the children in London during their early years. When the family moved to Bristol, naturally she came with them. We're told that Molly was an old-fashioned sort who *"thrived"* on wages of £10 a year.[171]

One of Dr Pole's most intimate and poignant drawings shows Molly in the hallway at 14 St James Square, about to go upstairs with a pot of tea and cakes for her ailing mistress. It's among dozens of pictures crafted by the doctor that appear as illustrations in Wedmore's biography. Dr Pole was a fine draughtsman, with a deft artistic touch and a good eye for detail, perhaps enhanced further by his skills as a surgeon.

Thomas and Betsy enjoyed over 20 years together in Bristol, mainly happy ones, until she died from cancer in 1823. Her husband nursed her through a long and painful final illness. Dr Pole's own death followed in 1829, peacefully, at the age of 75.

Silhouettes by Dr Thomas Pole of himself and his wife Elizabeth Pole ("Betsy"), 1804.

Sarah Champion Fox's continuing ill health had forced her to give up writing the treasured Diary at the end of 1802. In one of her very last entries, on 29 December, she left a fulsome and emotional tribute to Dr Pole and family.

"The frequent intercourse I had with Dr Pole, his wife & family, as well as my frequent visits to the Summer House & garden, once our own, greatly added to my comfort as I found both the doctor and his wife truly religious, valuable & kind neighbours, & as parents ruling their family well – not by a rod of iron, but by affection. For though early trained to habits of obedience, they were uncommonly attached to father and mother, who...took care to go hand in hand on everything which respected their children, who were well deserving their love." [172]

Sarah Champion Fox was to live on for almost another decade. But she called time on her Diary on New Year's Eve - 31 December 1802 - with this message for posterity:

"I think it is now time to put an end to this journal, as advanced age and increased infirmities have, in my own opinion, disqualified me for its continuance - never having felt so forcibly the wise man's assertion that 'there is nothing new under the sun;' & that I can generally now express only the same sentiments and feelings - and perhaps nearly in the same words." [173]

Then, eventually, Sarah's own turn came to be "removed". She died on 11 November 1811, at home in Brunswick Square, when in her seventieth year.

Dr Pole himself wrote an elegant obituary, which appeared in the *Public*

Advertiser three days later. It said his friend had *"possessed from early life a mind highly cultivated by education, extensive reading, & intercourse with the enlightened and pious from several denominations."*

Dr Pole continued: *"All who enjoyed the pleasure of her cheerful, as well as instructive, society, will acknowledge that in her, the characters of the Christian & gentlewoman were exhibited with peculiar gracefulness.*

"Her charities were bounded only by the extent of her fortune: they were bestowed, without a shadow of ostentation, on numerous private objects whose sufferings came to her knowledge, & claimed her benevolence & sympathy; the many who participated in her liberality will long have cause to lament the loss of so hospitable a benefactress." [174]

Dr Pole's wise words still resonate in today's divided and troubled world. The lives of Sarah Champion Fox and our dissenting Georgian doctors proved that being religiously devout needn't make you narrow-minded. Given wide-ranging education, books and conversation, plus tolerance of other faiths, you could be both pious and enlightened.

CONCLUSION

Pills, Shocks & Jabs started off as a biography of one eighteenth century man who was an amateur doctor and also happened to be a Quaker. Shurmer Bath was fascinating in his own right, but not enough to sustain a whole book. It soon morphed into a wider exploration of Quakers and other religious dissenters as an influential minority in Bristol. They often chose medicine as a career path, in order to skirt round establishment prejudice and help deliver better healthcare for the "deserving poor".

Being a retired journalist, my approach has been different from that of some academic historians with more detailed knowledge. I wasn't looking for information to fit a particular scenario or pattern. Instead, I followed a rambling trail suggested by the facts I came across and drew conclusions from what emerged. That learning process has left me in a constant state of wonder and surprise, which I think comes across in the narrative. What I discovered, for example, about early vaccinators and body-snatching surgeons wasn't always new, but it was certainly new to this author.

The doctors featured weren't all Quakers or other religious dissenters. For example, the apothecary Billy Broderip is included just because he was, apparently, such a notorious rogue. The Infirmary surgeon and chronicler, Richard Smith junior, is there because he told some of the best tales about individual colleagues. However, the book does show a common thread among Bristol Quakers, many of them choosing medicine at a time of limited career options.

They were barred from politics, local government and the military because of their pacifism and refusal to pledge allegiance to the King. However, Quakers could succeed in business or healthcare with fewer obstacles in their way. They also felt a strong moral pull towards helping weaker members of their community. Becoming an apothecary, surgeon or physician offered a way for dissenters to achieve this, while earning a decent salary to support them and their families.

The likes of Abraham Ludlow and Edward Long Fox worked exhaustingly long hours, but they also had the business acumen to profit from it and put the money to good use. Rich Quaker industrialists and merchants, who'd invested in iron, copper and coal mining to maximum effect, could transfer some of their profits into philanthropic causes linked to medicine.

In a healthcare system relying on charity, this gave the Champions, Harfords and other nonconformist grandees a degree of power and influence in the city that would otherwise have been denied them. Joseph Harford, in order to enter political life, had to leave the Quakers and join the established Church as an Anglican. He eventually became Mayor of Bristol in 1794. However, before that he held the post of Infirmary treasurer for 12 years. Other wealthy Friends manoeuvred their way into similar fundraising positions of influence.

Controlling the purse strings of a major charity, like the Infirmary, gave them some real clout in public life and a bigger say in Bristol's moral direction of travel. Quakers could earn the right to decide which patients to admit for treatment by being the main organisers and often most generous donors. They based these decisions, at least partly, on their own moral standards and judgment as to who constituted the "deserving poor".

The Quakers with a medic or two already in the family tended to be the ones who set up their own lucrative practice and took charge on the hospital wards. Some of them also later became the body snatchers who, contrary to all their religion stood for, showed a complete lack of respect for the dead in order to learn about dissection.

In a new century, the 1800s, Bristol's population was rapidly expanding, so dissenters formed an even smaller minority. As the total number of subscribers eligible to elect new hospital doctors increased, so Quaker power began to wane accordingly. They still had a big influence in a medical world still dominated by charity, but their glory days were coming to an end. Nevertheless, some healthcare achievement by Quakers - like new medical facilities, safer midwifery and better treatment for mental illness - endured to become their lasting legacy.

AFTERWORD

Writing a book on medical and social history was quite therapeutic in a long period of lockdowns caused by the coronavirus. In the midst of a pandemic, forcing the closure of libraries, museums and public archives, I did most of my research online from home.

Two centuries after her death, how would Sarah Champion Fox approach the Covid-19 era as a diarist? Would she have written a daily catalogue of Quaker lives lost to the virus? Or might she have focused on the small consolations, like a walk in the fresh air, meeting a friend or relative for a socially distanced chat, or a cup of tea in her garden?

I like to think the latter. Although matters of life and death always remained central to her thoughts, Sarah was never one for the big picture. She was well aware that lots of people were dying of smallpox, but didn't dwell on it. Instead, Sarah just mentioned in passing that she'd watched a doctor she knew, Abraham Ludlow, inoculating some children. End of story.

My way of coping in lockdown involved an escape route back to the 1700s, via my online research for this book, while keeping one eye on the news. How would our dissenting doctors react to the modern pandemic if they were still around?

Shurmer Bath would have subsidised the roll-out of vaccines through charity donations from the wealthy - offering free jabs to the poor and making the rest pay up. Dr Abraham Ludlow might be organising and giving the jabs. The apothecary Billy Broderip would charge everyone a fortune for a vaccine that didn't work. The psychiatrist Edward Long Fox might be treating people for the effect of the virus on their mental health.

Edward Jenner would perhaps be leading international co-operation to develop more vaccines against new variants of Covid. His cowpox experiments in the Georgian West Country seem especially relevant now, in the context of today's struggle to contain a modern global disease. We can still draw some inspiration from those enterprising medics of the eighteenth century.

ACKNOWLEDGEMENTS

Special thanks go to my wife Sue Cullimore for her invaluable help, particularly with final editing of the book. Sue offered love and a lot of patience while I was writing it, also expertise in the creative use of historical maps, from her career as a Geography teacher and university academic.

I sent our friend Linda Taylor each chapter of *Pills, Shocks & Jabs*, immediately it was done. As a retired college librarian with a passion for History, she was the ideal person to cast a very knowledgeable reader's eye over the text and give me her perceptive feedback at every stage along the way.

I'm grateful to another friend, Roger Ford of Know Your Place, for his guidance on map selection and illustrations of eighteenth century buildings, which he and colleagues have researched and put on their Bristol mapping website.

I'm also indebted to the academic historian Dr Madge Dresser for retrieving from obscurity *The Diary of Sarah Fox née Champion* a few years ago. A volume of extracts edited by her supplied a narrative thread linking the many Georgian Quaker medics who came into Sarah's social orbit.

Quaker local historian Roger Angerson, who's a former clerk to the Frenchay Meeting, ran a fact check over the book's references to Quakerism in the eighteenth century. His help was invaluable in ironing out some errors in my Quaker terminology.

A retired lawyer Roger Seddon, who's a friend from my student days, did me a generous favour. He spent many hours deciphering an historical legal document relating to Shurmer Bath's family.

There was an important contribution, too, from another historian in Bristol, John Penny. He kindly offered images of his great-grandfather's vaccination certificate, issued in 1858 and kept in the Penny family ever since. Thanks also to Clive Burlton, from my publisher Bristol Books, for telling me about it.

As with my previous book, I'm hugely impressed by the design talents of Joe Burt, also from Bristol Books. He again worked his magic to make *Pills, Shocks & Jabs* a pleasure to look at - as well as, hopefully, to read.

BIBLIOGRAPHY

Barry, Jonathan (editor), *The Diary of William Dyer: Bristol in 1762*, Bristol
Record Society, 2012

Barry, Jonathan, *Piety and the patient: Medicine and religion in eighteenth century
Bristol*, (Chapter Six of *Patients and Practitioners*, edited by Roy Porter),
Cambridge University Press, 1985

Best, G.M., *Slavery and Bristol*, New Room Publications, Bristol, 2020

Bertucci, Paola, *Shocking Subjects: Human Experiments and the Material Culture
of Medical Electricity in Eighteenth-Century England*, (chapter in *The Uses of
Humans in Experiment*, editors Erika Dyck and Larry Stewart), 2016

Bertucci, Paola, *The Shocking Bag: Medical Electricity in mid Eighteenth Century
London*, online paper, 2003

Bertucci, Paola, *Sparks in the Dark: the attraction of electricity in the eighteenth
century*, article in *Endeavour* journal, 2007

Boyston, Arthur, *Daniel Sutton, a forgotten 18th century clinician scientist*, article
in the *Journal of the Royal Society of Medicine*, 2012

Brunton, Deborah, *Pox Britannica: Smallpox Inoculation in Britain 1721-1830*,
PhD dissertation, University of Pennsylvania, 1990

Camp, Anthony, *Apprenticeship* article in *Practical Family History*, no 64, April
2003

Chandler, J.H., *Wiltshire Dissenters' Meeting House Certificates and Registrations
1689-1852*, Wiltshire Record Society, Devizes, 1985

Clark, Joanna, *Quaker Silhouettes*, article in *The Friend* magazine, July 2011

Cullimore, Peter, *Saints, Crooks & Slavers: History of a Bristol House and its
People*, Bristol Books, 2020

Davenport, Romola Jane, *Urban Inoculation*, online article, *The Economic
History Review*, Vol 69, Issue 1, February 2016

Dresser, Madge, *Slavery Obscured: the Social History of the Slave Trade in
Bristol*, Redcliffe Press, 2007

Dresser, Madge (editor), *The Diary of Sarah Fox née Champion 1745-1802*,
Bristol Record Society, 2003

Fissell, Mary, *Patients, Power and the Poor in Eighteenth Century Bristol*,
Cambridge University Press, 1991

Fry, David, *The Fry Family Tree*, Frenchay Village Museum, 2016

Haines, Robert, *The Ludlows of Chipping Sodbury*, article in *Gloucestershire History* No.6, 1992

Harvey, Charles; Press, Jon, *Studies in the Business History of Bristol*, Bristol Academic Press, 1988

Ingram, Allan, *Patterns of Madness in the Eighteenth Century*, Liverpool University Press, 1998

Latimer, John, *The Annals of Bristol in the Eighteenth Century*, Bristol, 1893

Levinson, David, *Body Snatching*, article in *Encyclopaedia of Crime & Punishment*, SAGE Publications, 2002

Mackintosh, Alan, *Rethinking Georgian Healthcare: The Patent Medicines Industry in England 1760-1830*, PhD dissertation, University of Leeds, 2015

Malony, H. Newton, *John Wesley and the Eighteenth Century Therapeutic Uses of Electricity*, American Scientific Affiliation, 1995

Manco, Jean, *History of St Peter's Hospital*, on Bristol Past website, 2006

Matthews, William, *Matthews's New Bristol Directory for the Year 1793-4*, Bodleian Libraries collection, University of Oxford. Also available at Bristol Central Reference Library

Moon, Robert, *The Morris Family of Philadelphia Descendants of Anthony Morris 1654-1721*, Vol 4, Philadelphia, 1908. Also available on Ancestry website.

Neve, Michael, *Natural Philosophy, medicine and the culture of science in provincial England: the cases of Bristol 1790-1850*, PhD dissertation, University of London, 1984

Pead, Patrick, *Benjamin Jesty: the first vaccinator revealed*, article in *The Lancet*, December 2006

Pelling, Margaret, *The Apothecary as Progenitor*, Cambridge University Press, 1983, published online 2012

Perry, C. Bruce, *The Bristol Medical School*, Bristol branch of the Historical Association, 1984

Perry, C. Bruce, *The Voluntary Medical Institutions of Bristol*, Bristol branch of the Historical Association, 1984

Rees, Charlotte, preface by Shurmer Bath to *Sermons*, 1796

Russell, James, *Repton & the Rich Apothecary: New Light on Cote Bank*, Avon Gardens Trust Journal No.1, summer 2006

Russell, Mortimer, *Early Bristol Quakerism 1654-1700,* Bristol branch of the Historical Association, 1967

Schiffer, Michael, *Draw the Lightning Down: Benjamin Franklin and Electrical Technology in the Age of Enlightenment,* University of California Press, 2003

Sketchley, James, *Sketchley's Bristol Directory of 1775,* Kingsmead Reprints Bath, 1971. Also available at Bristol Central Reference Library

Smith, G. Munro, *A History of the Bristol Royal Infirmary,* J.W. Arrowsmith Ltd, 1917

Smith, Leonard, *A gentleman's mad-doctor in Georgian England: Edward Long Fox and Brislington House,* from *History of Psychiatry,* Sage Publications, 2008

Sommers, Susan, *The Siblys of London,* Oxford University Press, 2018

Taylor, Kay Shelly, *Society, Schism and Sufferings: the First 70 years of Quakerism in Wiltshire,* University of the West of England, unpublished PhD thesis, 2006

Uglow, Jenny, *In These Times: Living in Britain Through Napoleon's Wars 1793-1815,* Faber & Faber, 2014

Wedmore, Edmund Tolson, *Thomas Pole M.D.,* Headley Brothers, 1908.

Wesley, John, *The Desideratum: or, Electricity Made Plain and Useful, by a Lover of Mankind and of Common Sense,* Bristol, 1760

Wesley, John, *Journal 1735-1790,* Moody Press Chicago, 1951

Wright, Mary, *Montpelier – a Bristol Suburb,* Phillimore & Co, Chichester, 2004

Whitfield, Michael, *The Dispensaries: Healthcare for the Poor before the NHS,* AuthorHouse, 2016, or Google Books

Wilson, Gaye, *Inoculation* article in *Thomas Jefferson Encyclopaedia,* 2004

ENDNOTES

Chapter 1: Dr Bath of Bristol

1   Clark, Joanna, *Quaker Silhouettes*, article in *The Friend* magazine, July 2011
2   *Sketchley's Bristol Directory of 1775*
3   Moon, Robert Charles, *The Morris Family of Philadelphia Descendants of Anthony Morris 1654-1721, vol 4*, 1908, p. 116
4   Ditto, p109
5   Draft conveyance, Bristol Archives, 5918/20
6   Stokes Croft Character Appraisal, Bristol City Council, 2007
7   Latimer, *The Annals of Bristol in the Eighteenth Century*, p. 2
8   Quaker Births, Marriage and Death Records, on Ancestry website.
9   *The Morris Family of Philadelphia family archive*, p. 110
10 Quaker Records
11 Cullimore, Peter, *Saints, Crooks & Slavers: History of a Bristol House and its People*, 2020, p. 15
12 London Apprenticeships Abstracts 1442-1850, on Ancestry
13 Camp, Anthony, *Apprenticeship* article in *Practical Family History, no 64* (April 2003), pp. 12-14
14 Smith, George Munro, *A History of the Bristol Royal Infirmary*, 1917, p. 32
15 London Clandestine Marriage and Baptism Registers 1667-1754

Chapter 2: "Quakerville"

16 *Sketchley's Bristol Directory of 1775*
17 *Mathews' Bristol Directory 1793*
18 Pelling, Margaret, *The Apothecary as Progenitor*, 1983, p. 52
19 *The Diary of Sarah Fox née Champion 1745-1802*, edited by Madge Dresser, 2003, p. 243
    Wedmore, Edmund Tolson, *Thomas Pole M.D.*, 1908, p. 30
20 Russell, Mortimer, *Early Bristol Quakerism 1654-1700*, 1967, p. 10
21 Harvey, Charles; Press, Jon, *Studies in the Business History of Bristol*, 1988, pp. 46-49
22 Russell, Mortimer, *Early Bristol Quakerism*, p. 21
23 Fissell, Mary, *Patients, Power and the Poor in Eighteen Century Bristol*, 1991, pp. 6-7
24 Neve, Michael, *Natural Philosophy, medicine and the culture of science in provincial England*, 1984, p. 219
25 Bristol Museums & Galleries Collections website (online narrative about Blind School)
26 *The Diary of Sarah Fox*, p. 135
27 Ditto, p. 182
28 Rees, Charlotte, preface by Shurmer Bath to *Sermons*, 1796
29 *The Monthly Magazine*, September 1800, p. 198
30 Draft conveyance Reeve/Bath, Bristol Archives, 5918/20
31 Lease of Ashley Cottage, Bristol Archives, 42165/1

Chapter 3: Fry's Healthy Chocolate

32 *The Diary of Sarah Fox*, p. 8
33 Ditto, Introduction, pp. x-xii
34 Joseph Fry family tree, Ancestry website
35 *The Fry Family Chocolate Makers*, from Quakers in the World website
36 Fry, David, *The Fry Family Tree*, 2016, p. 24

37 *The Diary of Sarah Fox*, p. 10
38 Ditto, p. 10
39 Ditto, p. 10
40 Ditto, p. 97
41 Ditto, p. 98
42 Ditto, p. 98
43 Smith, Leonard, *A gentleman's mad-doctor in Georgian England: Edward Long Fox and Brislington House*, from *History of Psychiatry*, 2008, p. 166
44 Ditto, p. 166
45 *The Diary of Sarah Fox*, pp. 104-105
46 *The Morris Family of Philadelphia family archive*, p. 111
    Notes on Quaker Births, Marriage and Death Registers, on Ancestry website
47 Dresser, Madge, *The Diary of Sarah Fox*, Introduction, p. xix
48 Taylor, Kay Shelly, *Society, Schism and Sufferings: the First 70 Years of Quakerism in Wiltshire*, 2006
49 Fry, David, *The Fry Family Tree*, 2016,

Chapter 4: Shurmer Bath's Restorative Pills

50 British Newspaper Archive website
51 Cullimore, Peter, *Saints, Crooks & Slavers*, 2020, pp. 13-14

Chapter 5: Desperate Remedies

52 Barry, Jonathan, *Piety and the Patient: Medicine and Religion in Eighteenth Century Bristol*, chapter from *Patients and Practitioners*, editor Roy Porter, pp. 145-175
53 Barry, Jonathan (editor), *The Diary of William Dyer: Bristol in 1762*, 2012
54 Fissell, Mary, *Patients, Power and the Poor in Eighteenth Century Bristol*, 1991, p. 40
55 Barry, Jonathan, *Piety and the Patient: Medicine and Religion in Eighteenth Century Bristol*, chapter from *Patients and Practitioners*, editor Roy Porter, p. 152
56 Fissell, Mary, *Patients, Power and the Poor*, p. 40
    Mackintosh, Alan, *Rethinking Georgian Healthcare: The Patent Medicines Industry in England 1760-1830*, 2015, p. 55
57 *The Diary of William Dyer*, p. 102
58 Ditto, pp. 151-152
59 Smith, G. Munro, *A History of the Bristol Royal Infirmary*, pp. 249-251
    Fissell, Mary, *Patients, Power and the Poor*, pp 49-56
60 Smith, G. Munro, *A History of the Bristol Royal Infirmary*, p. 251
61 Ditto, pp. 252-255
62 Russell, James, *Repton & the Rich Apothecary*, 2006, pp 2 - 5
63 Sommers, Susan, *The Siblys of London*, 2018, p. 60
64 Ditto, pp 61-63
    Pelling, Margaret, *The Apothecary as Progenitor*, 1983, p. 52
65 Smith, G. Munro, *A History of the Bristol Royal Infirmary*, p. 254
66 *The Diary of Sarah Fox*, p. 55
67 Fissell, Mary, *Patients, Power and the Poor*, pp. 64-65
68 Pelling, Margaret, *The Apothecary as Progenitor*, p. 52
69 Virol, *Food for Health*, St Margaret's community website, London, November 2016.
70 Wills, via Prerogative Courts of Canterbury records published on Ancestry website

Chapter 6: Bright Sparks

71 *The Diary of Sarah Fox*, p 63
72 Schiffer, Michael Brian, *Benjamin Franklin and Electrical Technology in the Age of Enlightenment*, 2003, pp 135-143
73 Bertucci, Paola, *Sparks in the Dark: the attraction of electricity in the eighteenth century*, article for *Endeavour journal*, 2007, p. 89 and online
74 Bertucci, Paola, *The Shocking Bag: Medical Electricity in mid Eighteenth Century London*, online paper, p. 2, 2003
75 *The Diary of Sarah Fox*, p. 77
76 Dresser, Madge, Introduction to *The Diary of Sarah Fox*, p. xix
77 *The Diary of William Dyer*, p. 106
78 Bertucci, Paola, *The Shocking Bag*, pp 2-5
79 Barry, Jonathan, Introduction to *The Diary of William Dyer*, p. 27
80 *The Diary of William Dyer*, p. 146
81 Ditto, p. 157
82 Ditto, p.159
83 Ditto, p. 169
84 Barry, Jonathan, *Piety and the Patient: Medicine and Religion in Eighteenth Century Bristol*, from *Patients and Practitioners*, editor Roy Porter, pp. 154-155
85 Ditto, pp. 155-156
86 *A Short History of the New Room* from the New Room Bristol website
87 Maloney, H. Newton, *John Wesley and the Eighteenth Century Therapeutic Uses of Electricity*, from *Perspectives on Science and Christian Faith*, 1995
88 Wesley, John, *Journal 1735-1790*, p. 138
89 Ditto, p. 218
90 Wesley, John, *The Desideratum*, 1760, pp. 43-70
91 Ditto, pp 42-43
92 Ditto, p. 71
93 Fissell, Mary, *Patients, Power and the Poor*, p. 10
94 Maloney, H. Newton, *John Wesley and the Eighteenth Century Therapeutic Uses of Electricity*, 1995, p. 3
95 Sommers, Susan, *The Siblys of London*, 2018, pp 63-64
96 Fissell, Mary, *Patients, Power and the Poor*, p. 25

Chapter 7: The Georgian Scourge

97 Davenport, Romola Jane, *Urban Inoculation*, article in *The Economic History Review*, 2016, p. 188
98 Jenner Institute website, University of Oxford
99 Ditto
100 Pead, Patrick, *Benjamin Jesty: the first vaccinator revealed*, article in *The Lancet*, December 2006
101 Haines, Robert, *The Ludlows of Chipping Sodbury*, Gloucestershire Local History Association, 1992
102 UK Register of Duties Paid for Apprentices Indentures 1710-1811, Ancestry website
103 *The Diary of Sarah Fox*, p. 25
104 Brunton, Deborah, *Pox Britannica: Inoculation in Britain 1721-1830*, University of Pennsylvania, 1990, p. 10-17
105 Jenner Institute website, University of Oxford
106 Brunton, Deborah, *Pox Britannica: Inoculation in Britain 1721-1830*, p. 98-126
107 *The Diary of Sarah Fox*, p. 25
108 Boyston, Arthur, *Daniel Sutton a forgotten 18th century clinical scientist*, article in the *Journal of the Royal Society of Medicine*, 2012
109 Smith, G. Munro, *A History of the Bristol Royal Infirmary*, p. 252
110 Brunton, Deborah, *Pox Britannica: Inoculation in Britain 1721-1830*, p.103-105

111 Wilson, Gaye, *Inoculation*, article in *Thomas Jefferson Encyclopaedia*, 2004
112 The Health Foundation website, Policy Navigator section

Chapter 8: Pauper Hospital

113 Manco, Jean, *History of St Peter's Hospital*, on Bristol Past website, 2006
114 Ditto
115 Smith, G. Munro, *A History of the Bristol Royal Infirmary*, pp. 117-119
116 Ditto, p. 99
117 Ditto, p. 115
118 Ditto, p. 118
119 Ditto, p. 118
120 *The Diary of Sarah Fox*, pp 71-72
121 Whitfield, Michael, *The Dispensaries: Healthcare for the Poor Before the NHS*, 2016, Chapter 2
122 Neve, Michael, *Natural Philosophy, medicine and the culture of science in provincial England: the cases of Bristol 1790-1850*, 1984, pp. 241-250
123 Quaker Records
124 Neve, Michael, *Natural Philosophy, medicine and the culture of science in provincial England*, p. 241
   Perry, C. Bruce, *The Voluntary Medical Institutions of Bristol*, p. 7
125 *The Diary of Sarah Fox*, p.216, p. 233
126 Smith, G. Munro, *A History of the Bristol Royal Infirmary*, p. 195
127 Perry, C. Bruce, *The Voluntary Medical Institutions*, p. 8
128 *The Diary of Sarah Fox*, pp. 27-28
129 Ditto, p. 31
130 Ditto, p. 121-122
131 Smith, G. Munro, *A History of the Bristol Royal Infirmary*, p. 119
132 Fitch family tree on Ancestry website

Chapter 9: Body Snatchers

133 Levinson, David, *Body Snatching*, article in *Encyclopaedia of Crime and Punishment*, 2002
134 Smith, G. Munro, *A History of the Bristol Royal Infirmary*, p. 206
135 Ditto, pp. 208-209
136 Ditto, p. 207
137 Levinson, David, *Body Snatching*, 2002
138 Smith, G. Munro, *A History of the Bristol Royal Infirmary*, pp 210-212
139 Ditto, p. 203

Chapter 10: Bristol Infirmary

140 Bristol Live (Bristol Post) website
141 Smith, G. Munro, *A History of the Bristol Royal Infirmary*, pp. 26-32
142 Neve, Michael, *Natural Philosophy, medicine and the culture of science in provincial England*, p. 226.
143 Smith. G .Munro, *A History of the Bristol Royal Infirmary*, pp. 427-428
144 Ditto, p. 184
145 Ditto p. 429-430
146 Ditto, p. 19
147 Ditto, pp 266-267
148 Ditto, p. 266
149 *The Diary of Sarah Fox*, p. 11
150 Russell, Mortimer, *Early Bristol Quakerism*, p.19
   Quaker Records
151 Fry, David, *The Fry Family Tree*
   Quaker Records

Chapter 11: Madhouse Doctor

152 Smith, Leonard, *A gentleman's mad-doctor in Georgian England: Edward Long Fox & Brislington House*, chapter from *History of Psychiatry*, 2008, pp 165-166

153 *The Diary of Sarah Fox*, numerous references

154 Dresser, Madge, *Slavery Obscured*, 2007, p. 139

155 Latimer, John, *The Annals of Bristol in the Eighteenth Century*, 1893, p.503

156 Smith, Leonard, *Edward Long Fox & Brislington House*, p. 168

157 Ditto

158 Ditto, p. 169

159 Ditto, pp 170-179

160 *Report From The Committee on Madhouses in England, 1815*

161 Ingram, Allan, *Patterns of Madness in the Eighteenth Century*, 1998, p. 246

Chapter 12: Polar Attraction

162 *The Diary of Sarah Fox*, p. 238

163 Ditto, pp. 242-243

164 Wedmore, Edmund Tolson, *Thomas Pole M.D.*, 1908, p. 30

165 *The Diary of Sarah Fox*, p. 234

166 Ditto, p. 166

167 Ditto, p. 241

168 Wedmore, Edmund Tolson, *Thomas Pole M.D.*

169 Smith, G. Munro, *A History of the Bristol Royal Infirmary*, p. 371

170 Wedmore, Edmund Tolson, *Thomas Pole M.D.*, p. 31

171 Ditto, p. 41

172 *The Diary of Sarah Fox*, p. 250

173 Ditto, p. 251

174 Ditto